Writing to the Point

Sixth Edition

Writing to the Point

Sixth Edition

Allan Metcalf
MacMurray College

Birch
Grove
Publishing

Writing to the Point, Sixth Edition
Allan Metcalf

Library of Congress Catalog Card Number: 93-80891

Manufactured in the U.S.A.
1   2   3   4   5   6   7   8   9   10   11   12   13   14   15

Preface to the Sixth Edition

It works. It really works. Good writers learn to write better; struggling writers learn to write well, by following the method taught in this book. It is a method, not a gimmick; it requires attention and thought; but it really works.

The quickest way to confirm this is to see for yourself. Skip the rest of this front matter, turn to Chapter 1, Step 1, and get started. You will soon see what a difference it makes.

But if you'd like a little explanation:

The method works because it fits the way our minds work and the way our language works. And because it teaches by example.

This book focuses on one thing at a time, step by step—six steps in all, from the beginning idea to the finished theme. That's the way our minds work, focusing on one thing at a time. Even better, the six steps are connected, one leading to the next. That's the way we learn, not by trying to absorb dozens of different instructions all at once, but taking them one at a time.

Furthermore, this focus makes use of the way we naturally express ourselves in language. When we communicate, our language consists not of isolated individual words but words combined into sentences; not just topics but comments about topics (subjects and predicates, to be technical). The method of this book begins likewise, with a sentence, a topic and comment, not just a topic alone. That's Step 1: Write a sentence. There are a few conditions on the sentence, but that's the gist of it. It's the way we naturally communicate.

Finally, the book teaches by example. It not only

tells what to do in the six steps; better yet, it shows by plentiful examples what happens when you follow the steps. That too is how our minds work—we learn by example.

In fact, you've had an example right here, in the four preceding paragraphs. They don't exactly fit the six steps—real-life writing rarely does, as Chapter 10 will affirm—but they reflect the salutary lessons learned from the method. No one is too good a writer, or too poor a writer, not to benefit from these six steps.

Enough! On with the rest of the book, and see for yourself.

* * *

Special thanks to the late William J. Kerrigan, who invented this effective method some years ago, and to editor Paul Nockleby, who has been its champion for many years, first at Harcourt Brace Jovanovich and now at Birch Grove Publishing. And thanks also to countless students and colleagues at MacMurray College, who for many years have put this method to the test and helped refine it.

To the Instructor: An Essential Introduction

One bright morning a professor entered a college class-room, glanced at the class, and chalked these words on the board (yes, it was back in the days of chalkboards): "Write a sentence."

The professor was the late William J. Kerrigan, and that moment was the genesis of the method in this book. He turned from the board to register the stares and frowns of his freshman composition students. "Write a sentence," he declared, and paused again. "Make sure it is a sentence, not a topic or a title."

The class was silent, but Kerrigan was pleased to see eyes focusing on him and the three words. So he continued. "Write a short sentence. Write a simple sentence. Write a declarative sentence—one that makes a statement, not one that exclaims or commands or asks a question.

"Just write a sentence."

Silence hung in the room as breakfasts digested and the morning haze of sleep and headaches cleared. Note-books were opened, pens were extracted from pockets and bags. (Yes, those were the days of pen and paper.) "On a separate sheet of paper?" someone asked. "In ink?" asked another. "Should we double space?" asked a third.

Kerrigan calmly ignored these questions. He would specify those details later, but for now he wanted noth-ing to distract from his point. Quietly he looked around until pens, pencils, and paper were ready. Then he spoke again. "Write a short, simple, declarative sentence that makes one statement."

Another pause, and then another question. "Any kind of statement?"

This question was relevant. Kerrigan answered. "An opinion. An idea. A statement. Something you know about. Not simply a fact.

"Just do it," he added quietly.

And they did. They wrote sentences like "An old car is expensive to maintain" and "Cigarette smoking is dangerous to your health" and "Keats was a Romantic poet" and "Power corrupts."

"How about 'I can't think of a good sentence'?" asked one student. "Too hard," Kerrigan smiled in reply.

He asked students to read the sentences aloud. And then, pausing once more to make sure he had their attention, he explained:

"This is your thesis sentence, the main point of your essay. Everything else follows from it and supports it. You must keep not just to your topic but to the point you make about your topic."

As he continued his explanation, eyes began glazing over, attention began wandering back to breakfasts had, lunches planned, overdrawn bank accounts, letters in the mail. (Yes, those were the days of snail mail.) *A lecture is an effective way of displaying a professor's knowledge. A lecture is an inefficient way of learning.* (Two possible thesis statements, thought Kerrigan.)

So he stopped lecturing and instead gave another instruction. Eyes focused on him again. "Write three sentences about that first one. About the whole of it, not just something in it."

Pens went to work quickly this time. As pens began to pause, Professor Kerrigan waited for the next question.

"How can I write about the whole of the first sentence? I'm just repeating myself."

For the first time that morning, Kerrigan smiled, a smile of satisfaction. At last, a student who is thinking.

The question deserves a thoughtful answer.

"Explain your first sentence. Support it. Imagine someone is asking you what you mean, and doubting what you say. Show different ways in which your statement is true. Give your reasons."

And so it must have gone the day this method was born some years ago. A professor at a community college in California, with a lifetime of practical experience—Iowa-born and raised, trained for the priesthood, a secret agent in World War II, an insurance inspector, translator, and teacher of classical Latin and Greek—out of frustration with conventional approaches, invented the six-step method of expository writing presented in this little book.

What he taught was no different from what conventional wisdom sought to teach: Have a point to make, not just a topic to ramble about; keep to that point; support it with relevant evidence and details; make clear the connections among the parts of what you have to say. And also, unless there is some special reason to be devious, make your point clearly and directly.

All this is the stuff of every textbook and handbook on writing. But what these others lack, and what Kerrigan invented, was a method of ensuring that these principles would sink in, would become part of the writer's habits of thought and expression. Kerrigan set out not to write a textbook but to teach writing. So he was able to focus on the essentials: clear thought and orderly development. Perhaps he was inspired by his Jesuit and classical training to devise a method that would ensure clear and forceful development of ideas.

In any case, to many of those who followed Kerrigan's precepts, the six steps have been not only the best writing instruction they have ever encountered, but the only instruction that has significantly improved their writing.

Why it works, when other lessons to the same end do not, is perhaps a matter of psychology. It is impossible to pay attention to everything at once; we need a focus for our attention, and these six steps provide it. The method works because it concentrates on the learner's state of mind, rather than the instructor's. And it is helpful to writers of all degrees of skill—expert, average, and those who have difficulty writing—because it is explicit as well as focused; there is never an appeal to a mysterious "feel" for writing.

At a student's urging, Kerrigan wrote a full exposition of his method. It was first published in 1974 by Harcourt Brace Jovanovich as *Writing to the Point.* That book went through four editions, the last revised by me in 1987. A fifth edition, called *Essentials of Writing to the Point,* came out in 1993.

This little book, inspired by Kerrigan's original and informed by more than three decades of teaching the six steps, simply teaches the method, as clearly, directly, and briefly as possible. Each chapter presents one step and immediately illustrates it with examples. Each chapter then concludes with an assignment and exercises, because the method must be practiced, not just looked at or listened to. There are right and wrong answers, but no automatic ones; all require thinking.

Over the years it has become increasingly apparent that the Kerrigan method is concerned above all with the expression of ideas. Accordingly, in this version I have tried to focus more explicitly on the ideas underlying the original statements of the six steps, while retaining their pragmatic simplicity. The results aimed at in each of the six steps are the same as before, but the means, I hope, are more clearly set out.

Allan Metcalf
May 2008

Contents

Chapter 7: Style   84

The way something is written should reflect its meaning: form should follow function. Do not hesitate to repeat key words. Keep to the same grammatical subject. Achieve variety not by changing vocabulary but by making every third sentence or so noticeably longer than the others, and starting every third sentence or so with something other than the grammatical subject.

Chapter 8: Comparison and Contrast   93

In a contrast theme: 1. Make a specific Step 1 statement. Do not just say that two objects or persons are different; say what the basic difference is. 2. Select significant differences, not trivial ones. 3. Include only material that relates to the contrast. 4. If you mention something about one object or person, mention the same thing about the other. 5. Take up things in the order in which you first present them. 6. Indicate contrasts with connective words that signal opposite ideas.

Chapter 9: Argumentation: The Other Side   100

To consider two sides of an issue, conclude your theme with a paragraph that presents the best argument for the other side, followed by a paragraph that replies to that argument. Finish as usual with a rounding-off sentence that restates your point.

Chapter 10: The Real World   107

In all of your writing, follow each of the six steps, or have a reason for not doing so.

To the Student: What's the Point?

The six big steps in this little book are to be taken seriously. In fact, it is best to memorize them, because they are at the heart of expository writing—expository writing being the kind that makes and explains a point.

If you are making an effective point, you will be following the principles embodied in these six steps, whether you know it or not. The difference here is that you will know it. You will know exactly what to do to make an effective point, and exactly how to do it.

No mysterious feel for language is required, just the ability to write a sentence. That is why the six steps are useful for those who have had difficulty with writing, who get criticized for what they write without knowing how to make it better. The six steps tell exactly what to do to avoid criticism in the first place.

But then, on the other hand, there are those who are good writers by instinct, who generally receive praise for what they put on paper. They too will profit from learning the six steps by heart. Otherwise, if something they write isn't as persuasive as they wish, they too don't know how to improve it. If something goes wrong, they too don't know how to fix it. If their usually-praised writing gets criticized, they are devastated and helpless. I should know—I was one of those cases, until the six steps came along to provide backbone and understanding.

So in either case, the six steps are not optional touches to be applied during the course of this book and then forgotten. They are essential for good expository writing.

But they are not obvious. If they were, you wouldn't

need this book. They are not on the surface of good expository writing, but underlying it. The function of this book is to show what lies beneath the surface.

That is also why you will rarely find a published essay that on the surface exactly follows the six steps. I know—I've looked hard and found few examples. (Simple news stories in newspapers are among the few.) Real writers, including yourself on other occasions, will follow the underlying principles of the six steps, but will change the surface to accord with the particular kind of writing assignment. (That adjustment is discussed in Chapter 10.)

The six steps are like the exercises and drills performed by athletes in preparation for actual contests. They are like the layups and three-point shots practiced by basketball players, like the forehand and backhand practiced by tennis players, or like the keyboard and fingering techniques practiced by piano players. These fundamentals are essential to effective play in actual performance.

If you do not find the six steps obvious in every piece of expository writing you encounter, that is only because they are not always on the surface. Once you know the six steps, you will recognize them beneath the embellishments.

The six steps are so essential that even if you were trying to prove that good writing does not need them, you would have to use the six steps to make your point! To convince someone else that the six steps are not necessary, you would have to:

Step 1. Make that point: *The six steps are not necessary.*

Steps 2 and 3. Keep to that point, explaining how or why your point is true, and avoid drifting off the point to an irrelevant statement like **The *six steps are easy to learn.* (An asterisk indicates examples that are not satisfactory.)

Step 4. Provide specific, detailed evidence and explanation in support of your point.

Steps 5 and 6. Use appropriate connective words to make clear the flow of your argument.

Yes, it is indeed possible to inform or persuade a reader without following the six steps. But in order to persuade you that this is true, I would have to use the six steps. They are fundamental.

When you have learned them, you will not necessarily show them off. You will write themes, essays, reports, letters, evaluations and so on in their usual forms. But you will make unusually good sense, because you will know how to organize, focus, and support what you have to say; your writing will have unity, detail, and coherence.

So please turn the page, learn the first step, do what it says, and see what happens. A little practice, and you will be pleasantly surprised at the improvement. So will your friends, relations, instructors, employers, and significant others.

Chapter 1

Step 1: Making a Point

STEP 1: Write a sentence stating an opinion that will require further explanation.

You can read about the method for hundreds of pages, but, like exercise, it won't do any good unless you practice it. So here we switch from talk to practice. And the practice begins, very simply, with—

a sentence.

That is the essence of writing to the point: start with a point, a complete sentence, not just a topic.

We write to convey a message, to make a point. A complete sentence makes a point; a topic, by itself, does not.

A sentence tells something about the topic—what it is or was, does or did:

Someone } { is or was something.

Something } { does or did something.

For example (unsatisfactory examples are marked with an asterisk *):

Not just the topic: but the complete sentence:

*tomatoes   Tomatoes are easy to grow.

*weather   Weather affects people's moods.

*fences   Good fences make good neighbors.

If you find yourself with a topic, say something about it—write a sentence, make a point. That is how real-life communication proceeds. If someone mentions only a topic, the listener's natural reaction is to ask, What's the point?

Topic: Point (sentence) about the topic:

*dinner   Dinner was delicious.

*candles   Candlelight is romantic.

*baseball   Baseball strategy depends on percentages.

*life   Life is earnest.

It works equally well whether the subject matter is light:

My kitty is cute.

or heavy:

Aristotle misunderstood human physiology.

The sentence thus produced by Step 1 is not a title; it is the actual first sentence of a theme, the thesis or main point. A title is not necessary at all at this stage, but if there is a title it needs to be converted to a Step 1 sentence.

Title:	**Point (sentence) derived from the title:**
*Hermit Crabs	Hermit crabs make good pets.
*Advertising and Women	Advertising stereotypes women.
*Vulnerability of Children	Children are vulnerable.

Another possibility from that last title:

Children need protection.

As these examples show, titles do not have to translate word for word into Step 1 sentences. The question is always, what point does the writer want to make about the topic? And any one topic can have many possible points. For example:

Topic:	**Points (sentences) about the topic:**
*children	Children are a joy.
	Children are a heartache.
	Children are expensive.
	Children imitate their parents.

All of the examples given so far are of sentences that require further explanation. That is, it is possible in each case to imagine someone questioning the simple statement: Why do hermit crabs make good pets? How does advertising stereotype women?

Since the Step 1 sentence is an opinion, one topic may lead to opposite opinions, depending on the explanation the writer has in mind *(Jogging improves your health/Jogging harms your health)*. In fact, the best Step 1 sentences are those that can be challenged, those to which you can imagine intelligent opposition—a reader saying, What makes you think that's true? The point you make should be one you know about, one you believe to be true, and one for which you are ready to provide explanation and evidence.

Guidelines for the Step 1 Sentence

Since Step 1 guides the development of all the other sentences in the theme, it needs to be carefully chosen. Some additional guidelines will help in that choice. Later, when all six steps have been mastered, the reasons for these guidelines will be self-evident, and some of them will no longer be necessary. But for now, please make sure the Step 1 sentence meets all of these criteria:

1. The Step 1 sentence should be opinion or judgment, not simple fact. (Not *Dogs wag their tails* but *Dogs are friendly*. Facts come later, to support the judgment.)

2. The Step 1 sentence should require further explanation, prompting the reader to ask why or how it is true. (Not *Sunlight is bright* but *Sunlight relieves depression*.) As mentioned above, the best way to ensure this is to imagine someone saying the opposite—so that you will then have to explain why your view is true. Your Step 1 sentence does not have to be a matter of current controversy; it can be something that almost everybody believes, providing you can think of someone doubting it. Remember that little more than a century ago nearly everyone believed *A heavier-than-air vehicle cannot fly*, and little more than half a century ago nearly everyone believed *DDT is beneficial for the environment*.

3. The Step 1 sentence should be specific and focused, not general, so it is clear what kind of explanation will be required. (Not *Exercise is good for you*, but *Jogging strengthens the cardiovascular system*.) In your comment on a topic, avoid general words like *good, bad, important, great*. (Not *Broccoli is great*, but *Broccoli is nutritious*.)

4. The Step 1 sentence should avoid mere description, narration, or statement of a process. (Not *There were sixteen people in the room* but *The room was claustrophobic.* Not *Tying a bow requires five steps* but *Tying a bow is hard for a five-year-old.*) There will be plenty of room for description, narration, and process later, in Step 4.

5. The Step 1 sentence should avoid statements of personal preference, which also usually do not call for further explanation. (Not *I love chocolate* but *Chocolate stimulates romantic feelings.*) Avoid saying that something is *interesting* or *boring*, which really means it interests or bores you personally.

6. The Step 1 sentence should be a declarative sentence, making a statement rather than asking a question or giving a command. (Not *Why does it rain?* but *The cooling of clouds brings rain.* Not *Make up your mind!* but *Making up your mind can be difficult.*) It can, however, be the answer to a question. (What helps with a diet? *Reducing calories helps with a diet.*)

7. For now, the Step 1 sentence should be short and simple. (Not *Given the proper software, and with the exception of certain homographs, computers can eliminate spelling mistakes* but *Computers can eliminate spelling mistakes.*)

8. For now, The Step 1 sentence should make one statement, not more. (Not *Fly fishing requires practice and patience* but *Fly fishing requires practice* or *Fly fishing requires patience.*)

9. For now, The Step 1 sentence should avoid *should*—that is, it should avoid sermons about what should

be and tell what is. (Not *Everyone should eat broccoli* but *Broccoli helps the body resist disease.*) Inci-
dentally, that means the ten guidelines in this list
are not suitable Step 1 sentences.

10. For now, The Step 1 sentence should avoid comparison
    and contrast, because these require concentrating on
    several things at once. (Not *Men are more concerned
    with power than women are* or *Women are more con-
    cerned with intimacy than men are.* Not *Swimming
    is the best exercise,* which requires comparison with all
    other forms of exercise. Not *Computers have become
    more user-friendly,* because that involves comparing
    past with present. These complicating factors will be
    discussed in Chapter 8, where comparison and con-
    trast will be not just allowed but encouraged.)

Revising the Step 1 Sentence

As you proceed with Step 2 in the next chapter, you may
find that your Step 1 point needs modifying. That is fine;
in fact, you are encouraged to revise your point as you
develop your explanation of it and get a better understanding of exactly what you want to say. But it is essential from
the start not to wander pointlessly around a topic but to
begin immediately with a sentence, a complete statement,
however much it may need to be modified. So think; and
make a point. And then move on to Step 2.

Assignments and Exercises

At the end of each chapter, the assignments, like the
steps themselves, will eventually lead you to a complete
theme. The optional exercises will give you additional
practice.

Assignment 1

Following Step 1, write a sentence on a topic of your choosing, or a topic assigned by your instructor. Check the sentence to make sure it follows the guidelines given above. Be sure to choose a statement that requires further explanation (Guideline 2).

Exercises

Exercise 1.1. Write three possible Step 1 sentences for each of these topics: *children, television, cars, pets, plants, college, friends, money*. For example: *Children require attention, Television is relaxing*. Check the sentences to make sure they meet the guidelines for Step 1.

Exercise 1.2. For one sentence on each topic of Exercise 1.1, write a Step 1 sentence that expresses the opposite opinion. For example: *Children can take care of themselves, Television causes stress*.

Exercise 1.3. Write a possible Step 1 sentence for each of the following: a particular kind of food, a particular kind of car, a particular occupation, a particular kind of weather, a particular college course, a particular city or other place, a particular person you know.

Exercise 1.4. Choose the titles of three books, movies, or plays, and convert them to Step 1 sentences that suggest what the work is about. A few titles are complete sentences already (*The Mambo Kings Play Songs of Love*), but most will need an additional statement (*Pip has great expectations*, and *The things they carried reveal their personalities*.)

Exercise 1.5. Describe an object or person. Based on the description, write a Step 1 statement of opinion about that object or person.

Exercise 1.6. Tell a story about a person. Based on the story, write a Step 1 statement of opinion about that person.

Exercise 1.7. Write a list of your likes and dislikes. Use three of them as the basis for Step 1 sentences about what you like or dislike. Do not use *I* (Guideline 5), but focus on the subject or on your like or dislike. (For example, change *I like classical music* to *Classical music is relaxing.*)

Exercise 1.8. Write Step 1 sentences that answer the following questions (Guideline 6): a) How interested in politics are Americans? b) What do we learn from television? c) Why do people like ice cream sundaes? d) What do women want?

Exercise 1.9. Change the following Step 1 sentences so that they make only one statement (Guideline 8): a) *Raising a family is expensive and time-consuming.* b) *Stress leads to bad health, bad temper, and bad performance on the job.* c) *Eating one meal a day is a good way to diet and also saves a lot of time.*

Exercise 1.10. Restate the following so that they do not require contrast (Guideline 10): a) *Bicycles are more convenient than cars.* b) *Skis are better than snowshoes for cross-country travel.* c) *Frequent review of notes is the best way to study for a class.*

Chapter 2

Step 2: Explaining the Point

STEP 2: Write three or four additional sentences explaining how or why the Step 1 sentence is true or correct. To explain how, give examples, parts of the whole, sequence or chronology; to explain why, give reasons (causes).

If it took some time to explain the single sentence of Step 1, that is because the Step 1 sentence requires some thought. Step 2 calls for more thought, and more explanation.

But again the important thing is practice. Practice doing what Step 2 says, and you will never have trouble keeping to the point.

Here is the explanation: The sentence of Step 1 is the main point, or thesis sentence, of the entire theme. The Step 2 sentences are the main points, or topic sentences, of the three or four individual paragraphs of the theme. They must stick to the point, the whole of the Step 1 sentence, not just its topic. To do this without mere repetition, they explain the Step 1 sentence. They do this by giving examples, parts of the whole, sequence or chronology, or by giving reasons (causes).

Together, the Step 1 and Step 2 sentences form a sentence outline of the theme. To make the arrangement clear, let us mark the Step 1 sentence with an X, and put a number in front of each of the Step 2 sentences. Indent each sentence as at the start of a new paragraph. Here is an example.

X Children imitate their parents.
1. Children imitate their parents' actions.
2. Children imitate their parents' words.
3. Children imitate their parents' beliefs.

The sentence labeled X is the Step 1 sentence. The sentences numbered 1-2-3 are Step 2 sentences that use *examples* to develop the idea in sentence X. Actions, words, and beliefs are examples of the ways in which children imitate their parents. Here is another example of development by example:

X Emily Dickinson was a talented poet.
1. Her imagery shows her talent.
2. Her choice of words shows her talent.
3. Her unusual rhymes show her talent.
4. Her unusual punctuation shows her talent.

In this case, the "talented" of the Step 1 sentence is developed by example in the four sentences of Step 2, each being an example of a way in which she is talented. (Whether Step 2 uses three sentences or four, or even more, is left to the writer's judgment. Three, however, is the minimum.)

In the two examples so far, it is the statement about the subject ("imitate their parents," "was a talented poet") that has been made more specific by Step 2. Considering aspects of this statement (known as the predicate) is the most basic kind of Step 2 development. Here is one more example:

X The spelling of English words gives information about them.

1. It indicates how they are to be pronounced.
2. It indicates how they used to be pronounced.
3. It indicates what languages they came from.

Instead of developing the predicate, however, it is also possible to consider aspects of the subject in Step 2, as in this case of development by example or parts of the whole:

X Quincy, Illinois, is a beautiful town.
1. The downtown is beautiful.
2. The riverfront is beautiful.
3. The north side is beautiful.

Here it is the subject, Quincy, Illinois, that is considered in its different parts.

Another kind of Step 2 development, by *sequence or chronology*, involves following the stages of a process, or history, or the seasons. This is a way to involve a narrative or tell a story. However, by Step 2 the sequence or chronology is given not for its own sake but to explain the point of sentence X. For example:

X Painting a room requires care.
1. Preparing the room for painting requires care.
2. Applying the paint requires care.
3. Cleaning up afterwards requires care.

X Vacations are enjoyable year round.
1. Vacations are enjoyable in the spring.
2. Vacations are enjoyable in the summer.
3. Vacations are enjoyable in the fall.
4. Vacations are enjoyable in the winter.

X Chicago has always been a forward-looking city.
1. Chicago was a forward-looking city when it was founded in the 1830s.

2. Chicago was a forward-looking city at the time of the World's Fair of 1893.

3. Chicago was a forward-looking city at the time of the Century of Progress fair of 1933.

4. Chicago is a forward-looking city today.

So far this chapter has illustrated the development of Step 2 by examples, parts of the whole, sequence or chronology. But it is also possible for Step 2 to *explain why* sentence X is true, by giving *reasons* or *causes*. For example:

X Good fences make good neighbors.

1. Good fences keep plants from spreading into neighbors' yards.

2. Good fences keep animals from straying into neighbors' yards.

3. Good fences protect neighbors' privacy.

X Chocolate is bad for you.

1. It rots your teeth.

2. It causes zits.

3. It is fattening.

A single Step 1 sentence may be developed in any number of directions. Here are several possibilities for the sentence *Commercial airline travel is safe.* First, using examples:

X Commercial airline travel is safe.

1. Travel on United Airlines is safe.

2. Travel on American Airlines is safe.

3. Travel on Delta Airlines is safe.

Then, with parts of the whole:

X Commercial airline travel is safe.

1. Commuter airline travel is safe.

2. National airline travel is safe.

3. International airline travel is safe.

With sequence or chronology:

X Commercial airline travel is safe.
1. Airline takeoff procedures are safe.
2. Airline in-flight procedures are safe.
3. Airline landing procedures are safe.

You need only three reasons, but you may have four or more):

X Air travel is safe.
1. Air travel is safe because of plane maintenance.
2. Air travel is safe because of emergency facilities.
3. Air travel is safe because of radar.
4. Air travel is safe because of pilot training.

(Another illustration of different ways of developing a single sentence X is in Appendix 2.)

Sometimes after Step 2 has been applied, it is apparent that Step 1 needs revision, that sentence X is not exactly what you meant to say. That's fine! Adjusting the Step 1 sentence to fit better is always appropriate. Take this example:

X Computers can do many things.
1. Computers can play chess.
2. Computers can analyze sentence grammar.
3. Computers can recognize voices.

Sentences 1-2-3 are examples of what computers can do, but are these really *many* things? They are only a few. Furthermore, "do things" is too general to fit the specifics of sentences 1-2-3. A more focused Step 1 sentence could be the opinion that *Computers can imitate human intelligence*, for which sentences 1-2-3 give examples.

You can find examples of Step 1 followed by Step 2 in professional writing. Here is a simple example by columnist Drew Pogge, writing in the *High Country News*:

I'm not a bad guy; I call my mother, eat my broccoli, and pay my taxes.

There is also a Step 1 followed by Step 2s in this paragraph by humorist Joel Stein, writing in *Time*:

> Touring wineries can make you feel like a jerk. Not just from saying that yes, you do totally taste the gooseberry in that merlot but also because the chemistry of oenology makes you feel stupid, the picking and crushing of grapes makes you feel wimpy, and the giant estates make you feel poor.

An important virtue of the six steps is that they require exactness of thought and expression. Careless thinking at one stage does not get past the scrutiny of the next. So Step 1 sentences that seemed fine at first may, on closer look, need improvement. And so it will happen when the Step 2 sentences encounter Step 3, and so on. The end result will be as clear, exact, and convincing a statement as possible.

A first attempt at Step 2 often needs improvement. Here are four examples, with explanations of how they can be improved.

a) X College classes are challenging.
   1. They require a lot of thinking.
   2. They require a lot of homework.
   3. They meet in the morning.

Problem: Sentences 1-2-3 should be ways in which college classes are challenging, but sentence 3 is not necessarily a challenge. *Solution:* Substitute for 3 something like *They require a lot of memorization.*

b) X Football practice is exhausting.
   1. You run until you're so tired you can hardly move.
   2. You drive people out of your way until your legs feel like rubber.
   3. Afterward you are so tired you don't feel like doing your homework.

Problem: Sentence 3 is not an aspect of football practice.
Solution: Substitute for sentence 3 something like *You have to lift weights until your arms are ready to fall off.*

c) X Oxygen is essential for life.
    1. It keeps trees alive.
    2. People need it to breathe.
    3. It is needed to start fires.

Problem: Sentence 3 is not a way in which oxygen is essential for life. *Solution:* Substitute for 3 something like *It is needed for water, an ingredient of all living things.* (Oxygen is not needed for trees in the same way it is for humans, but that is another story.)

d) X A job is important.
    1. Earning money from it is important.
    2. Responsibility is important.
    3. Learning what the public is like is important.

Problem: "Important" is too general and unfocused for Sentence X, so this set needs a complete makeover. *Solution:* Make a more specific statement in X and adjust 1-2-3 accordingly:

e) X A job is educational.
    1. It teaches responsibility.
    2. It teaches how to deal with the public.
    3. It teaches time management.

In most of the examples of this chapter, the Step 2 sentences repeat key words and sentence structure. They should, because they are repeating key ideas, and form should follow function: that is, similar ideas should be expressed in similar forms (See Chapter 7). Under these circumstances, repetition is not only permissible, it is desirable. The opportunity for variety will come in Steps 3 and 4, where the paragraphs headed by the Step 2 sentences are developed.

If you noticed other problems with the above exam ples than those explained here, good for you. The whole purpose of our six steps is to clarify and focus thinking. You can't do it on autopilot; at each step you have to think carefully. For example, you might well decide that *College classes are challenging* is much too general for a short theme. So it might be better to write about one particular class: *Calculus is a challenging course.*

Guidelines for Step 2 Sentences

A few additional guidelines will help ensure that the Step 2 sentences are ready for further development in the steps that follow.

1. The Step 2 sentences should not simply restate Step 1. They should explain it by stating ways in which sentence X is true, that is, by giving examples, parts of the whole, sequence or chronology; or by giving reasons for the statement in Step 1.

2. The Step 2 sentences should not overlap each other. Each Step 2 sentence should give a different aspect or a different reason.

3. The Step 2 sentences should not mix types of development. For any particular X-1-2-3, all Step 2 sentences should give examples, or all should give parts of the whole, or sequence or chronology, or reasons.

4. The Step 2 sentences should fit the Step 1 sentence as closely as possible. Adjust the Step 1 sentence if necessary for closer fit.

Assignment 2

For the sentence of Assignment 1 at the end of the previous chapter, write three or four sentences explaining it, following all the stipulations of Step 2. If necessary, revise the Step 1 sentence to fit the sentences of Step 2 better.

Exercises

Exercise 2.1. Write sets of Step 1-Step 2 sentences in X-1-2-3 form on these particular topics: today's weather, the most recent meal you ate, your current location.

Exercise 2.2. Write Step 1 sentences on the topics of fast food, computers, and clothes. For each, write three or four Step 2 sentences that focus on what is said about the topic, and arrange them in X-1-2-3 outline form. In each case tell what kind of development you have used—examples, parts of the whole, sequence or chronology, or reasons.

Exercise 2.3. Write Step 1 sentences on the topics in Exercises 1.1 and 1.3. For each, write three or four sentences by Step 2, and arrange them in the X-1-2-3(-4) outline form. Tell what kind of development you have used—examples, parts of the whole, sequence or chronology, or reasons.

Exercise 2.4. To each of the following, add a third Step 2 sentence that follows the development of the first two. Tell what type of Step 2 development it is.

a) X Television is a helpful learning tool.
   1. Television is a helpful learning tool in science.
   2. Television is a helpful learning tool in English.
   3. _____

b) X Television contains too much violence.
   1. Soap operas contain too much violence.
   2. Reality shows contain too much violence.
   3. _____

c) X Children are easily influenced.
  1. Children are easily influenced by their parents.
  2. Children are easily influenced by their peers.
  3. _____

d) X Six-year-old children are time-consuming.
  1. Feeding them is time-consuming.
  2. Giving them a bath is time-consuming.
  3. _____

e) X People enjoy their pets.
  1. People enjoy the attention their pets give them.
  2. People enjoy the devotion their pets give them.
  3. _____

Exercise 2.5. Write Step 2 sentences for each of these Step 1 sentences in the manner indicated:

a) Sequence or chronology: Getting a good grade on an exam requires careful preparation.

b) Reasons: Aerobic exercise is beneficial.

c) Examples: Owning a car is expensive.

d) Reasons: Owning a car is expensive.

Exercise 2.6. Each of the following sets does not meet the requirements of Step 2. In each case, explain what is wrong and then correct it.

a) X Airline travel is safe.
  1. Airline travel is comfortable.
  2. Airline travel is easy.
  3. Airline travel is fast.

b) X My brother is ambitious.
  1. He has three part-time jobs.
  2. He takes classes at night.
  3. His room is a mess.

c) X Going to college is fun.
1. You can learn a lot from college.
2. Going to college requires a lot of studying.
3. A college degree is very helpful.

d) X She is a compulsive shopper.
1. She once bought 49 boxes of cereal.
2. She has closets full of brand new shoes.
3. She never uses what she buys.

e) X Love can be expensive.
1. You have to buy too much.
2. You have to buy flowers.
3. You have to buy jewelry.

f) X Marriage is great.
1. A person to plan the future with.
2. A friend in time of need.
3. A person full of compassion.

(Hint: The most basic problem is grammatical.)

Chapter

3

Step 3: Completing the Point

**STEP 3: Write four or more additional
sentences about each of the three or four
sentences of Step 2. Conclude the theme
with a rounding-off sentence in a
separate paragraph.**

With Step 3, the outline provided by Steps 1 and 2 becomes
a complete theme. The challenge—and the opportunity—
is to keep to the point and develop it further, without
mere repetition.

When you have practiced this step, you will have
mastered the skill not only of making a point but of
keeping to it, despite all temptations to wander off. Yes,
there are three more steps after this, but with Step 3
the framework is fully in place.

Step 2 calls for development by examples, parts of
the whole, sequence or chronology, or reasons. Step
3 calls for similar development, but above all by *giving details* to explain the examples, parts of the whole,
sequence or chronology, or reasons presented in Step 2.
This matter of going into detail is so important that it

deserves a whole step to itself—Step 4, presented in the next chapter. In the meanwhile, the focus of Step 3 is keeping to the point.

Step 3 is also is where the expansion stops. Though there are more steps, there will be no more instructions to write additional sentences about the sentences of Step 3. So while it is useful to keep the sentences of Steps 1 and 2 fairly simple to allow for further development, the Step 3 sentences can be as rich and complex as desired without worrying about later complications.

Continuing an example from the previous chapter, Figure 3-1 presents a theme written according to the first three steps. Please use this format for all the themes you write from now *until the end of this course.* To make the outline clear, Steps 1 and 2 are presented by themselves at the outset, followed by a broken line. Then, below the line, the sentences of Steps 1 and 2 are repeated exactly, word for word, in the appropriate places and incorporated into the complete theme. This may seem strange, but there's a good reason for doing it exactly this way—so please do it.

X Children imitate their parents.
1. Children imitate their parents' actions.
2. Children imitate their parents' words.
3. Children imitate their parents' beliefs.

X Children imitate their parents.

1. Children imitate their parents' actions. For example, a child who is hugged by a parent will then turn around and hug a doll or a younger brother or sister. Likewise, a child who is hit by a parent will look for someone or something else to hit. A child whose parent drives above the speed limit will be likely to do the same

upon reaching driving age. A child whose parents smoke will likely take up the habit as a teenager.

2. Children imitate their parents' words. In infancy, they echo the baby talk their parents speak to them. As toddlers, they repeat whatever they hear, whether they understand it or not. In the preteen years, they adopt the accents and speech patterns of their parents. As teenagers, they may change their accent, but they will continue to repeat the words and phrases their parents use.

3. Children imitate their parents' beliefs. For example, if parents express belief in Santa Claus, their children will too. If the parents laugh at the notion of Santa Claus, so will the children. More importantly, children will echo the religious beliefs expressed by their parents. And whatever the parents believe about other races and cultures, so will the children.

So in all these ways, children imitate their parents.

Figure 3-1: Step 3 Theme

In the sample theme, each paragraph uses only one kind of explanation rather than switching to a different kind in midstream. The Step 3 sentences in paragraphs 1 and 3 are examples, as indicated by the introductory phrase "For example." Paragraph 2, however, uses the chronology of children's development from infancy to teen age. This different method of explanation makes paragraph 2 stand out from the others.

It is probably preferable to use the same kind of development for all Step 3 paragraphs; the first paragraph sets up a pattern with which the reader will be comfortable later. (See Exercise 3.1.) The kind of explanation used for Step 3 does not, however, have to be the same as for Step 2. For example, Step 2 can use reasons and Step 3 can use examples.

The Rounding-off Sentence

With Step 3, the outline has become a complete theme—simple and somewhat artificial-looking at this stage, but nevertheless making a point, keeping to that point, and developing it in detail. But if it were to stop with the last sentence of paragraph 3, the theme would end in a minor detail. So for a more satisfying ending, Step 3 also calls for a rounding-off sentence at the end: a restatement of Step 1 in light of the explanation that has been given.

Instead of the one in the Figure 3-1, the rounding-off sentence might touch on the subjects of the three main paragraphs: "So whether it is actions, words, or beliefs, in many ways children imitate their parents." In either case, with Step 1 at the start and a rounding-off sentence at the end, the theme begins and ends with the point.

(For a short theme, a conclusion consisting of a single sentence is ample, just as a single sentence X is sufficient for the beginning. A book or a twenty-page paper would require a full paragraph of introduction and another paragraph of conclusion, but for a one- or two-page theme, a single sentence at beginning and end is plenty.)

Figure 3-2 gives another example of a Step 3 theme. Step 2 gives reasons to support the statement in Step 1; Step 3 then gives examples and further reasons, all supporting the Step 1 point. After the third paragraph comes the rounding-off sentence, a one-sentence restatement of the theme in a paragraph by itself.

X A student can benefit from spending a year in a foreign country.
    1. She can learn practical skills.
    2. She can discover a new way of life.
    3. She can benefit personally from the experience.

X A student can benefit from spending a year in a foreign country.

1. She can learn practical skills. Without the help of parents or friends she must take care of the details involved in traveling from one country to another. Once she arrives, she has to learn how to use the public transportation system to get around. She must learn to manage her own money and possessions. With hard work she can even master a foreign language.

2. She can discover a new way of life. She learns that the climate is not like ours. Holiday celebrations seem unusual by her standards. Strange new sights are everywhere, and people's behavior seems embarrassing at times. Even prejudice, she discovers, is different, because it is based on social class, not color or race.

3. She can benefit personally from the experience. Living with another family can teach her to compromise. Accepting other people's differences and difficulties will make her tolerant. She will have a wider perspective for moral and ethical judgments. She can mature a great deal as a result of making her own decisions and handling her own life.

In skills, knowledge, and personal development, then, a student has much to gain from living abroad.

Figure 3-2: Second Step 3 Theme

The examples given so far show Step 3 properly applied. That is, every sentence keeps to the point established by Sentence X. But what happens when a theme slips off the point? Figure 3-3 gives an illustration of how a theme slips off the point. This third example has acceptable Steps 1 and 2, but serious problems with Step 3.

X Holidays are exciting.
1. The Fourth of July is exciting.
2. Thanksgiving is exciting.
3. Christmas is exciting.
4. New Year's is exciting.

X Holidays are exciting.

1. The Fourth of July is exciting. It is the day we celebrate the birth of our nation. For well over two centuries it has been a day to remember. Cities and towns, large and small, have celebrations. Many businesses are closed for the Fourth of July.

2. Thanksgiving is exciting. Gathering relatives together from distant places makes for an exciting reunion. For example, a person might be excited to see a newborn nephew or niece for the first time. Toddlers are excited at the large crowd of people. At the first Thanksgiving hundreds of years ago it was probably the same.

3. Christmas is exciting. The season of Christmas brings a thrill to everyone's heart. The enthusiasm is contagious. Everyone is animated.

4. New Year's is exciting. It is not just one day, but the night before. Some people go out while others stay home. Some make noise while others watch the noise on television. People make resolutions for the new year.

Figure 3-3: Theme with Step 3 Problems

In this theme, Step 2 keeps to the point, using examples of exciting holidays. But Step 3 does not. If you can tell what's wrong, you have learned the lesson of this chapter. Briefly:

Paragraph 1 keeps to the topic but not to the point; its sentences say nothing about the excitement of the holiday.

Paragraph 2 is the most difficult case. Individually, its sentences meet the requirements of Step 3; each one does explain the Step 2 sentence, including excitement as well as the Thanksgiving holiday. The problem is that each develops the Step 2 sentence in a different way. First comes a reason, then an example, then parts of the whole (toddlers as compared with those of other age groups), then what might be the first element of a chronology. As mentioned above, it is best to have one kind of explanation for all instances of Step 3 in the entire them (it need not be the same kind as for Step 2), and it is certainly necessary to have one kind of explanation for the Step 3 instances in a particular paragraph.

Paragraph 3 keeps to the point, but it too has a problem. It merely repeats the point rather than developing it. Furthermore, paragraph 3 has only three Step 3 sentences, one less than the minimum.

Paragraph 4, like paragraph 1, gets off the point. It says nothing about New Year's being exciting.

Finally, there is no rounding-off sentence. As it stands, Figure 3-3 ends with people making new year's resolutions, which is far from the original point.

It may be objected that professional writers do not keep so rigorously to the point as Steps 1, 2, and 3 require. True; in real writing there is more leeway for digression. But professional writers know when they drift from their point, and why. They have good reasons for making exceptions, some of which will be discussed in Chapter 10. Meanwhile, it is important to master what the professionals already know. At this stage what is needed is practice in keeping to the point.

Some professional writing does keep strictly to the point. Here is a paragraph from an astronomy magazine:

As late as 100 years ago, people tenaciously believed that the lunar orb was a substantial determinant of human affairs. Charles Darwin wrote that the gauchos of South America did nothing unless the moon was right. Moreover, immediately prior to the French Revolution, the government directed its foresters to cut timber only "in the wane of the moon." Alexander Graham Bell was so convinced that the moon's "magnetic forces" influenced his health that he covered the windows in his home in order to block out the rays of a full moon. Charles Dickens was equally concerned with magical "pullings." [Perry W. Buffington, *Sky*.]

This professional writer uses a more elaborate style, but he develops his paragraph in the same manner as the sample themes of this chapter.

That is enough for a start. Since Step 4 is so important for Step 3, we will give only one assignment and two exercises here, saving the full development for the chapter that follows.

Assignment 3

For the sentences of Assignment 2 at the end of the previous chapter, write additional sentences as stipulated in Step 3. If necessary, revise the sentences of Steps 1 and 2 to fit the Step 3 sentences better. Follow the exact format of the examples in this chapter, writing the Step 1 and 2 sentences as an outline, then drawing a line, then writing the complete theme incorporating the Step 1 and 2 sentences with Step 3. Double space so there will be room for corrections and comments. Finish with a rounding-off sentence recapitulating the point in a paragraph by itself.

Exercises

Exercise 3.1. Rewrite paragraph 2 of the sample theme on children (Figure 3-1) so that it uses the same kind of explanation as paragraphs 1 and 3—examples rather than chronology.

Exercise 3.2. Correct the theme in Figure 3-3.

Chapter
___
4

Step 4: Going into Detail

STEP 4: Go into detail in the four or more sentences of Step 3. Make them as specific as possible. Make them concrete. Use examples and facts. Say a lot about a little, not a little about a lot.

Step 4 requires the most detailed treatment of all, because that is what Step 4 is about: going into detail to support the point and subpoints expressed in Steps 1 and 2. That is easily enough said, but (to show how necessary Step 4 is) it has to be demonstrated by going into detail, or the instructions will remain unclear.

Of all the six steps, Step 4 is the most fundamental to all kinds of good writing—and perhaps the hardest. It is relatively easy to make a point, much harder to provide the details to support it. Too often writers leave that hard work to their readers, as if the readers are ready to do hard work that the writers wouldn't. *Children imitate their parents,* we casually say, without bothering to provide a shred of evidence; another time we can just as easily say that *Children avoid their parents' example.*

How do we expect someone to believe either of these assertions? By going into detail—Step 4.

Step 4, it must be emphasized, does not mean writing additional sentences about the sentences of Step 3. Instead, Step 4 tells how to write those Step 3 sentences—what to put in them so that they avoid mere repetition while keeping to the point.

The essence of Step 4 is its first three words: *Go into detail.* The rest of Step 4 tells specific ways to do this.

A. Being Specific

The first specific instruction of Step 4 is to be specific. But what, specifically, does *specific* mean? The opposite of *specific* is *general*, but there is no exact dividing line between general and specific—it is more of a scale, ranging from *thing* or *something* at the most general end to a very particular item at the most specific. So, for example:

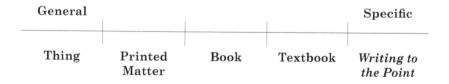

General			Specific
Thing	Printed Matter	Book	Textbook	*Writing to the Point*

In this example, *printed matter* is more specific than *thing*, *book* is more specific than *printed matter*, and *textbook* is more specific than *book*. We cannot be satisfied with *printed matter*, because that is too general; Step 4 says that the sentences of Step 3 are to be *as specific as possible*. So we must go all the way, to the title of the specific book. In fact, we could get even more specific, and say *a well-worn copy of* Writing to the Point, *lying open to page 45*. That would be an appropriate detail to support a thesis claiming that a certain person was studious.

Note that, in being specific, you can use as many words as you need. Here is another example:

General				Specific
Person	Author	American author	African-American author	Zora Neale Hurston

A particular person is as specific as you can get. If the particular person is not known to the reader, however, more than the name will be necessary in order to be as specific as possible. For example:

General				Specific
Person	State Employee	Illinois Historical Preservation Agency Employee	Director of Public Information, IHPA	David Blanchette, Director of Public Information, IHPA

Each move to the right is more specific. A state employee is a particular kind of person, an Illinois State Historical Agency employee is a particular kind of state employee, and so on. Step 4 asks that you make the sentences of Step 3 as specific as possible—all the way to the right.

Note that this instruction applies just to the sentences of Step 3. Steps 1 and 2 need to be more general; in applying Step 4, leave them alone.

Being specific is essential to the business of living. At a restaurant, we cannot be general and order "food, please"; we have to choose specific items from the menu—the mixed greens salad, for example—and sometimes even have to specify how we want them served: "oil and vinegar dressing; yes, thank you, a little fresh pepper."

We cannot turn to a friend and say, "Hand me something, please." Instead, we have to be specific about the thing: "Pass me that ball-point pen—no, I mean the red one with the cap." That is Step 4. *Thing* or *something* won't do. They are too general.

Being specific is especially important in writing about people. In giving opinions, we are likely to refer to a worker, *a student, a parent, a traveler—*or even the most general of all, *a person.* That is acceptable for Steps 1 and 2, but not for the sentences of Step 3. Step 4 says that the sentences that fill out the paragraphs need to get down to specific supporting instances, as specific as possible. So for example, instead of the general term a worker, the writer needs to specify a particular kind of worker: *a restaurant worker*, or more particularly *a kitchen worker in a restaurant,* or more particularly *a cook at the Original Pancake House.*

Likewise, a Step 3 sentence about *a student* is not specific enough. Specify the kind of student: *a college student,* or more particularly *a college sophomore,* or more particularly *a sophomore taking Political Science 203, American Government, at 8 a.m.*

As in the previous example of the state employee, one way to be as specific as possible about people is to name a particular person—provided the reader will know who the person is. Otherwise, the way to be specific is to give relevant specifics: *a 27-year-old computer systems engineer who teaches UNIX and C programming language.*

A specific sentence is like a sharp photograph; it enables the reader to see the details. Is the Step 3 sentence *She wrote in ink* specific enough? No, it needs a more detailed picture: *Holding the pad in her right hand, with a blue medium Paper Mate Write Bros. ballpoint pen in her left she wrote the order in a bold looping script.*

If a Step 3 sentence reports what someone said, then to follow Step 4 and be as specific as possible is to use the person's exact words: a direct quotation instead of a paraphrase. For example (again, the unsatisfactory version is marked with an asterisk *):

> *Shakespeare said love doesn't kill people. / Rosalind, the heroine of Shakespeare's *As You Like It*, says to her overly romantic lover, "Men have died from time to time and worms have eaten them, but not for love."

Here are other examples of Step 3 sentences that are not specific enough, changed to make them more specific.

> *Terry is young. / Terry is barely 7 years old.

> *The shipment is heavy. / The sixteen crates of oranges weigh 330 pounds.

> *They grew lots of vegetables. / In a plot measuring 40 feet square, they grew broccoli, bush beans, cabbage, celery, corn, onions, peas, potatoes, radishes, and tomatoes.

Is it possible to do too much? Is there no end to being specific? Yes there is, if we keep Step 3 in mind. Step 3 calls for sentences that support the opinion expressed in Step 1, so it allows only those details that support the point. It is like making a case in court, or ordering in a restaurant; details are needed (Step 4), but the details must be relevant (Step 3) In a restaurant, to order *an appetizer* is not specific enough; you must tell the server you want *the Bavarian chips*. But if in addition you wish to discuss the terrain where the potatoes were grown for the chips, or the freight car in which they were shipped, the server will be puzzled. Those specifics are not relevant, so by Step 3 they should not be there. By Step 4, though, the specifics that are relevant should be as specific as possible.

Professional writers take care to be specific too. Instead of writing *He looked like a Byzantine icon*, Dan Hofstadter wrote this specific description for *The New Yorker:*

> He had a way of tilting his head back as he spoke, so that his eyes, foreshortened, became almonds, and his mustache turned into a perfect arch, and his beard expanded and grew blacker, more velvety. His sort of face shown against a light background formed the principal problem of the old icon painters, which was to give the modeling of a very dark head against a nimbus of gold. Comb his hair with an eggbeater, throw a camel skin over his shoulder, and Bearded Ahmet would have made a perfect John the Baptist. (*The New Yorker*)

B. Being Concrete

Step 4 also demands that the Step 3 sentences be as concrete as possible. Things are either *concrete* or *abstract;* there is no sliding scale as there is for general and specific. Concrete things are things properly speaking, while abstract things are thoughts about things. But the way to test for concrete is this: If you can see, hear, touch, smell, or taste something—if you can perceive it with one or more of your senses—it is concrete. If not, it is abstract.

So a table, a shoe, a sock, a pizza, and a person are concrete; the sun, the moon, the earth, a star, a planet are concrete; a speck of dust and the roar of a jet engine are concrete; the smell of fresh coffee is concrete; all plants and animals are concrete. A flag, a forest, a grain of sand, a dollar bill, a recording of a song—all are concrete. Any object is concrete, if you define an object as something you can see or touch (or hear or smell or taste).

The opposite of *concrete* is *abstract*, the realm of ideas. These, for example, are abstract: *happiness, fear, sincerity, old age, art, neatness, philosophy, love* and *hate, success* and *failure, beauty* and *ugliness, fashion, health, nutrition, excitement* and *boredom, entertainment,* even *life* and *death.* In Steps 1 and 2 we use abstractions like these to express our ideas, our interpretations of concrete reality (although the term *reality* itself is an abstraction). As we provide support for the ideas in Steps 3 and 4, we must be concrete: a smile for *happiness,* an open palm for *sincerity,* a scream for *fear,* a withered face for *old age,* a painting or poem for *art,* an orderly desk or room for *neatness,* a book (or Socrates) for *philosophy,* a heart for *love* and a dagger for *hate.* A flag can stand for the abstract notion of *patriotism*; a ballot box for the abstract idea of *democracy,* a chain for *slavery,* and so on.

Here are more examples. *Beauty* is abstract, but a beautiful picture is concrete; *strength* is abstract, but a strong man or woman is concrete; a *happy expression* is abstract, but a smile is concrete; *love* is abstract, but *a kiss* is concrete. Concrete does not mean that it is hard like concrete; it just means that you can taste, smell, touch, hear, or see it.

Often a concrete representation is a person associated with an abstraction: a doctor for *health* (or *sickness*!), a banker (or professional athlete) for *wealth*, an actor for *entertainment*. As Shakespeare explained long ago:

Such tricks hath strong imagination,
That, if it would but apprehend some joy,
It comprehends some bringer of that joy.

Joy is abstract. So to make it comprehensible, we imagine someone who brings joy: a musician, a magician, a good friend. That is what Step 4 requires.

Animals (which are always concrete) can stand for abstract human characteristics: a donkey for *laziness*, a monkey for *mischievousness*, a cow for *contentment*, a sheep for *docility*.

It is not concrete to say you can see the *anger* in someone's expression. What you can see is the frown, the narrow lips, spread nostrils, red flush in the skin, throbbing veins, jaw thrust forward, fists clenched. That the person is angry is an interpretation, an idea, suitable for Steps 1 or 2; the details of the Step 3 sentences provide the concrete support for this interpretation.

Sometimes a word can be abstract or concrete, depending on the way it is used. The sports of *basketball, football, baseball, volleyball* are abstract, for example, but the basketball, football, baseball, volleyball used in those sports are concrete and often serve as symbols of them.

A particular symbol can stand for more than one idea. A flag can symbolize *war* as well as *patriotism*, for example, or it can symbolize *nationalism, victory, or dedication*. (That is why we sometimes argue about the flag.) And a given abstraction, like *peace*, can have many possible symbols, such as a dove, an olive branch, or a white flag. Your reader will know what connections you want to make between abstract and concrete because you will be stating the abstractions in Steps 1 and 2 and linking them with the concrete examples in the sentences of Steps 3 and 4.

The strength of writing to the point is not just the abstract general opinions, nor just the concrete specific details, but the connection between them—the use of the latter to support the former.

C. Using Examples and Facts

One of the best ways to go into the detail required by Step 4 is to use examples. Of course, the examples you offer should be detailed, specific, and concrete (Step 4)—and to the point (Step 3).

They should also be real examples, not hypothetical ones. This is for two reasons. First, a hypothetical example is not convincing. If your Step 1 point is *Watching violence on television encourages children to be violent,* but your Step 4 example is *After watching a violent cartoon, a preschool boy may hit his brother*, the reader is likely to ask, "Do you have an actual example of this happening?"

The second reason for avoiding hypothetical examples is that they tend to be general rather than specific, as in the preceding example. The reader will ask, What cartoon? What specific violence? What kind of hitting? So have an actual example in mind, and give the details.

Examples are so effective, in fact, that one sure way to satisfy Step 4 is to start the second sentence of each paragraph with the words *For example.*

In addition to examples, the other kind of material suitable for Step 4 is facts. It may be a fact that within the city the speed limit is 35 miles per hour unless otherwise posted, or that a cup of cooked broccoli has only half a gram of fat, or that the Gettysburg Address has 280 words. If certain facts provide evidence to support your Step 1 point, they belong in your Step 3 sentences. Again, they should be specific: to say that cars must drive slowly in the city, or broccoli is low in fat, or the Gettysburg Address is short, is not to be as specific as possible. Some facts require research; a paper whose Step 3 sentences are based on research instead of personal or general knowledge is known as a research paper.

D. A Lot About a Little

If you are writing a book, you can cover every possible aspect of the point you are making. In a short paper, you must be selective—especially if you are following Step 4 and being as specific as possible. An example may take more than one sentence to spell out in sufficient detail. In fact, it is entirely possible that a single relevant example may occupy all of the four or more Step 3 sentences that fill out a particular paragraph. If the choice is between too-brief mention of many possibilities and in-depth discussion of just a few, choose the latter. Say a lot about a little, not a little about a lot.

E. An Example

Figure 4-1 shows the sample theme of Figure 3-1, now changed to fit the requirements of Step 4. Note that the sentences of Steps 1 and 2 remain the same; Step 4 applies only to the sentences of Step 3 that fill out the paragraphs.

Note also that Step 4 has narrowed the focus of Step

3. In Figure 3-1, Step 3 was developed so that each paragraph had four subpoints. Adding Step 4 has reduced the first paragraph to two subpoints, the second to three, the third to just one. The reduction is a way of providing the necessary Step 4 depth—going into detail, saying a lot about a little—without increasing the length of the paper. (A longer paper could keep all of the Step 3 subpoints and develop each one.)

X Children imitate their parents.
1. Children imitate their parents' actions.
2. Children imitate their parents' words.
3. Children imitate their parents' beliefs.

X Children imitate their parents.

1. Children imitate their parents' actions. For example, when her mother, a teacher, sat down to grade papers, seven-year-old Agnes brought some sheets of notebook paper and her own red pen to the table and began scribbling in the margins and writing A's and B's at the top of the pages. When the mother took a break to get a glass of iced tea, the daughter also got up from the table and fixed her own glass with the same ice cubes and squeeze-bottle lemon (but no sugar) as her mother. Another example is that of three-year-old Susan, who sees her father drive home from work and then rushes out to the back yard where her battery-powered pink toy convertible is plugged in. She takes it gently around curves, remembering her father's own cautious driving.

2. Children imitate their parents' words. For example, one-year-old Arnold's vocabulary included the words *mama, dada,* and *kitty,* all of which his parents had endlessly said to him. The word *kitty* at first was a simple *ee* sound, but it developed into *kee*

and eventually *kitty* as he attempted to sound like his parents. At age two, Arnold was trying to say *orange juice*, but it came out *ainu*. With continued effort to sound like his parents, in another year or two he was saying *orange juice*.

3. Children imitate their parents' beliefs. For example, thirteen-year-old Barbara shares her parents' beliefs about the environment. She calls her friend Kiki and says of her neighbors, "Aren't they gross? They don't even recycle their aluminum cans but just put them in the trash. And I heard them laughing about our compost pile. It's disgusting. If adults won't take care of the environment before it's too late, who will?" Earlier that evening, at a dinner of vegetable stew cooked in the solar oven, her mother and father had said the same thing about the neighbors. "The city should refuse to collect their trash," said her mother. "It's disgusting."

So whether it is actions, words, or beliefs, in many ways children imitate their parents.

Figure 4-1: Step 3 theme revised by Step 4

Assignment 4

Revise the theme you wrote for Assignment 3 at the end of the previous chapter so that the sentences in the paragraphs follow Step 4 while staying on the point. Add words to sentences and sentences to paragraphs wherever appropriate, so that each paragraph is at least 100 words long. Double space and follow the format of the examples given in this chapter and the previous one.

When you have finished adding Step 4, consider each addition in the light of Step 3. If it is not clearly related to the point, throw it out or explain its relevance.

Exercises

Exercise 4.1. For each of the following general words, fill in four additional stages towards being as specific as possible, as illustrated earlier in the chapter. Use the form given for the first example below. Do not hesitate to increase the number of words as you get more specific.

General   Specific

Tree

General words to use:

1. tree	5. furniture	9. money
2. game	6. view	10. clothes
3. picture	7. gift	11. shelter
4. car	8. food	12. flower

Exercise 4.2. Think of one or more concrete representations of each of the following.

1. success	12. sincerity	23. fact
2. failure	13. courage	24. education
3. ugliness	14. cowardice	25. poverty
4. fashion	15. wisdom	26. government
5. health	16. skill	27. law
6. nutrition	17. competition	28. religion
7. excitement	18. stress	29. business
8. boredom	19. reconciliation	30. advertising
9. entertainment	20. enjoyment	31. marketing
10. life	21. confusion	32. understanding
11. death	22. fiction	33. invisibility

Exercise 4.3. Make the concrete representations you wrote for Exercise 4.2 more specific, using the pattern of Exercise 4.1.

Exercise 4.4. Think of concrete representations for the seasons: spring, summer, fall, winter.

Exercise 4.5. Think of concrete representations for different sports and games: soccer, tennis, golf, badminton, chess, Monopoly.

Exercise 4.6. Think of concrete representations for different fields of study: science, mathematics, biology, chemistry, physics, literature, philosophy, history, economics, journalism, astronomy, engineering.

Exercise 4.7. Think of concrete representations for the seven deadly sins:

1. pride   4. lust   6. gluttony
2. avarice   5. wrath   7. sloth (laziness)
3. envy

Exercise 4.8. Change the italicized words and phrases in the following sentences to make them as concrete and specific as possible. There are many possible ways of doing each. You will need to increase the number of words.

A. She put *an object* in the bookcase.
B. The *pet* ate its *dinner*.
C. *He* gave the waiter *a look*.
D. *Exercise* takes *time*.
E. *The American* brought *a gift* for *her hostess*.
F. *Television* teaches *lessons*.
G. Here is *a thing* that will look good in your *collection*.
H. *She* went to *the store* to pick up *certain items*.
I. *He* ate *his food* with extreme carefulness.

Exercise 4.9. Write a paragraph full of Step 4 detail that begins with the Step 2 sentence *My drawer is neat* (or *My drawer is messy*).

Exercise 4.10. Write a paragraph full of Step 4 detail that begins with the Step 2 sentence *The view was beautiful.*

Exercise 4.11. How could Step 4 be applied to the theme about living in a foreign country presented of Chapter 3? Point out specific places in Figure 3-3 needing revision before comparing it with the Step 4 version (Figure 4-2) below. (Note that the changes of Step 4 have led to a revised, more specific Step 1 sentence as well.)

X A student can benefit from spending a year in Brazil.
1. She can learn many practical skills.
2. She can discover a new way of life.
3. She can benefit personally from the experience.

X A student can benefit from spending a year in Brazil.

1. She can learn many practical skills. Without the help of parents or friends she must deal with customs agents, handle a passport, enroll at a new school, and conquer the public bus system. Managing her money and possessions might be new for her, but with effort she can learn to do her own laundry, organize her books and papers, and balance her checkbook. If she is efficient and thrifty, she can learn to make $175 last a month. With hard work she can even master Portuguese.

2. She can discover a new way of life. She will find that, since the seasons are the opposite of ours, the temperature is over 110 degrees on Christmas day. The holiday seems strange to her anyway, because instead of a big dinner at home, everyone visits friends and goes from house to house drinking wine and eating. Poverty is a fact of life in Brazil, she will learn, so it is common to see children begging on the streets. Some customs are

so different they seem embarrassing to an American; for example, teenage girls hold hands when they walk down the street, the way small children do in this country. Even prejudice, she discovers, is different: racially mixed couples are common, but a person from the upper class cannot marry a person from the lower class without being disowned by his or her family.

3. She can benefit personally from the experience. By living with a new family, she will have to learn to compromise when she wants to study or shop and the mother is sick and needs help. A student who sees begging children daily develops not only compassion, but also judgment, since she has to decide which one is trying to sell her a ribbon and which one is going to grab her money and run away. She will always have a second reference point in addition to her native one when making decisions about her personal morality. Being accepted by the Brazilians can give the student a better feeling about herself than being accepted by her own kind.

In skills, knowledge, and personal development, then, a student has much to gain from living abroad.

Figure 4-2: Step 3 theme revised by Step 4

Exercise 4.12. In the sample theme of Exercise 4.11, point to places where it the writer could be still more specific. What kinds of additional examples or details would make the writer's point clearer?

5

Step 5: Key Connections

STEP 5: Change the first sentence of each new paragraph, starting with paragraph 2, so that it connects with the paragraph before it. Add key words to connect topics and connective words to connect ideas.

With Step 5 we enter the realm of the professional writer. A good amateur piece of writing will follow Steps 1 through 4, making a clear point and supporting it in detail. That will do for many situations. But professionals know that one more stage is needed to make the writing polished and clear. That stage is connections—Steps 5 and 6. They guide the reader through the theme, so that the point is not only made but fully understood.

Step 5 connects one paragraph to the next; Step 6, the subject of the next chapter, connects one sentence to the next.

Because it covers more territory, Step 5 makes a more important connection than Step 6. But both steps have the same function. They inform the reader of the logical relationship between one statement and the next.

Both steps employ the same methods—*key words* and *connective words*. (Step 6 allows other methods as well, as will be explained in the next chapter.)

Key words are words that identify main topics. It is not only permissible but desirable to repeat key words for emphasis, as in Abraham Lincoln's "of the people, by the people, for the people" or Martin Luther King, Jr.'s repeated "I have a dream." In Step 5, we look for the key word or words that identify the main topic of one paragraph and add them to the start of the next. Words that are important enough to be the key words of a paragraph are usually found in the Step 2 sentences that provide the paragraph topic sentences.

Connective words are words whose chief function is to connect other words and ideas. They are especially important in making clear the development of the point—because a theme has a point, not just a topic.

The choice of connective words depends on the kind of relationship between the points of the different paragraphs. Since there are several possible kinds of relationships, there are several kinds of connective words. The next chapter will discuss seven of these kinds: addition, example, identity, opposite, cause and effect, concession, and focusing. But here we will not have to get so complicated, because the simple examples we have used so far have used just one of the kinds: addition.

When the relationship between paragraphs is one of addition, it means simply that the new paragraph provides additional explanation; it states something in addition to (and in agreement with) what has already been stated. This is the most frequent kind of connection, not just in a six-step theme, but in all writing. It uses connective words like *and, also, too, additionally,*

*in addition, moreover, likewise, similarly, furthermore,
as well as, along with, another, again, besides, in the
same way; not only . . . but also.*

Adding Step 5 to a theme changes it in only a few
places. Step 5 affects only the second paragraph and
those following it. In each of those paragraphs it changes
only one sentence—the first.

To avoid obscuring the basic points, Step 5 changes
are made only in the actual paragraphs, not in the Steps
1 and 2 outline at the start of the theme. Here is an
illustration of how Step 5 operates, using the theme on
children's imitation from previous chapters. The Step 5
changes are indicated in **bold type**.

X Children imitate their parents.
1. Children imitate their parents' actions.
2. Children imitate their parents' words.
3. Children imitate their parents' beliefs.

X Children imitate their parents.

1. Children imitate their parents' actions. For example, when her mother, a teacher, sat down to grade
papers, seven-year-old Agnes brought some sheets of
notebook paper and her own red pen to the table and
began scribbling in the margins and writing A's and B's
at the top of the pages. When the mother took a break to
get a glass of iced tea, the daughter also got up from the
table and fixed her own glass with the same ice cubes
and squeeze-bottle lemon (but no sugar) as her mother.
Another example is that of three-year-old Susan, who
sees her father drive home from work and then rushes
out to the back yard where her battery-powered pink
toy convertible is plugged in. She takes it gently around
curves, remembering her father's own cautious driving.

2. Children imitate **not only their parents'** **actions but also** their parents' words. For example, one year-old Arnold's vocabulary included the words *mama, dada,* and *kitty,* all of which his parents had endlessly said to him. The word *kitty* at first was a simple *ee* sound, but it developed into *kee* and eventually *kitty* as he attempted to sound like his parents. At age two, Arnold was trying to say *orange juice,* but it came out *ainu.* With continued effort to sound like his parents, in another year or two he was saying *orange juice.*

3. **In addition to their parents' words**, children **also** imitate their parents' beliefs. For example, thirteen-year-old Barbara shares her parents' beliefs about the environment. She calls her friend Kiki and says of her neighbors, "Aren't they gross? They don't even recycle their aluminum cans but just put them in the trash. And I heard them laughing about our compost pile. It's disgusting. If adults won't take care of the environment before it's too late, who will?" Earlier that evening, at a dinner of vegetable stew cooked in the solar oven, her mother and father had said the same thing about the neighbors. "The city should refuse to collect their trash," said her mother. "It's disgusting."

So whether it is actions, words, or beliefs, in many ways children imitate their parents.

Figure 5-1: Step 5 Added to Step 4 Theme

The number of sentences changed by Step 5 will always be one less than the number of paragraphs in the theme. In this example, since there are three paragraphs (aside from the Step 1 sentence at the beginning and the rounding-off sentence at the end), the number of sentences changed is two.

The first change comes in Sentence 2. To connect topics, we must add to it a key word or words that refer to the main topic of the previous paragraph. That paragraph deals with *parents' actions,* so those are the key words added to Sentence 2 at the start of the second paragraph.

As for connecting ideas with connective words, looking back at paragraph 1, paragraph 2 provides an additional way in which children imitate their parents, so words indicating that addition are appropriate for Sentence 2: *not only . . . but also.* With key words and connective words added, the revised version of the sentence that starts paragraph 2 then reads: *Children imitate not only their parents' actions but also their parents' words.*

At the start of paragraph 3, the Step 5 changes work in a similar way. The key words that distinguish the topic of the previous paragraph are *their parents' words;* the connection of ideas again is something in addition to the previous paragraph, that is, one more way in which children imitate their parents. It is possible, if a writer wishes, to use not just one but two connectives, as happens in this paragraph with both *in addition to* and *also.* The revised first sentence of paragraph 3 thus reads: *In addition to their parents' words, children also imitate their parents' beliefs.*

To take another example, consider the Step 4 theme of Exercise 4.11, dealing with the benefits of spending a year in Brazil. The original sentence 2 says *She can discover new ways of life.* Step 5 calls for the addition of key words from the previous paragraph, whose topic is *practical skills;* it also calls for connective words to connect the ideas, and paragraph 2 connects with paragraph 1 by giving an additional reason for the student benefiting. So a revised sentence 2 could read: *In addition to learning practical skills, she can discover new ways of life.* Or it could be more elaborate: *Aside from learning practical skills, another reason she will benefit from a year in Brazil is that she can discover new ways of life.* Sentence 3 of that theme could be developed similarly (see Exercise 5.2).

Step 5 does not add any more sentences to a paragraph; it changes a sentence that is already there. But the original sentence should not be changed beyond recognition. It is important to keep the emphasis on the original Step 2 statement, so that the reader will not be misled into thinking that the new paragraph is merely a restatement of the previous one. The new Step 5 material should be grammatically subordinate, leaving the original Step 2 as the main statement.

It is also generally helpful for the Step 5 additions to come at or near the beginning of the changed statement. That puts them close to the previous paragraph, the one they refer to. In turn, it leaves the original Step 2 statement at the end of the changed sentence so it can directly lead to the rest of the paragraph.

Since Step 5 shows the connections of topic and idea from one paragraph to the next, it requires the writer to think about those connections, revise them if necessary, and express them as precisely as possible. Are the three or four sentences of Step 2 arranged in the most logical and lucid order? If so, make that order clear; if not, rearrange them and then make the new order clear. Connective words that express "in addition" are perfectly satisfactory in most cases, but the careful writer can be more precise. For the theme on children, here are possible Step 5 sentences making closer connections than those given earlier:

2. *Just as they watch their parents' actions, children also listen to* their parents' words *and* imitate *them.* . . .

3. *As they grow older,* children *progress from simply mimicking* their parents' *words to agreeing with the* beliefs *expressed by those words*.

As these examples show, many different connections

are possible in Step 5. The same is true for the sentence-to-sentence connections of Step 6. The next chapter, dealing with those connections, will also further explain the variety possible for Step 5.

Assignment 5

Add Step 5 to the theme you wrote for Assignment 4 at the end of the previous chapter. Make the Step 5 changes only below the line, so that the X123 outline at the start of the theme remains clear and simple. Change only the first sentence of each new paragraph, starting with paragraph 2; add key words to identify the topic of the immediately preceding paragraph and add connective words to clearly and precisely indicate the development of ideas from one paragraph to the next.

Then ask yourself if the three or four sentences of Step 2, and their associated paragraphs, are arranged in the most logical and systematic order. If so, use Step 5 to make that arrangement clear. If not, rearrange the paragraphs and then use Step 5 to make the revised arrangement clear.

Exercises

Exercise 5.1. In the theme on children imitating their parents, the Step 5 key words added in paragraph 2 must include the topic *actions* and in paragraph 3 must include the topic *words*, as in the example. But in connecting the ideas, different connective words could be used. For example, paragraph 2 could begin, _Furthermore, children imitate their parents' actions as well as their words._ Keeping to the instructions of Step 5, and changing the connective words but not the key words, give two other possible forms for the first sentence of paragraph 2 in that theme, and three other possible forms for the first sentence of paragraph 3.

Exercise 5.2. Apply Step 5 to the start of paragraph 3 of the Step 4 theme on studying in Brazil. See Exercise 4.11 and this chapter's discussion of that theme's paragraph 2.

Exercise 5.3. In the following theme, which sentences need to be changed in applying Step 5? Find them and apply it.

    X Football is warlike.
1. Football employs warlike clothing.
2. Football employs warlike armies.
3. Football employs warlike generalship.
4. Football employs warlike hand-to-hand combat.

    X Football is warlike.

    1. Football employs warlike clothing. The most striking example of warlike clothing is the helmet all players wear. Like a soldier's helmet in war, the football helmet is padded on the inside and hard on the outside to protect the wearer's head from enemy assault. Like a soldier's helmet, it covers the ears and the back of the neck as well as the top of the head. The bars across the face of a football helmet recall the face guards of helmets in medieval warriors' armor.

    2. Football employs warlike armies. A football team of eleven men led by a quarterback is the same size as an infantry squad led by a staff sergeant. A football team deploys platoons for offense and defense and specialized squads for kicking and punting, just as the military has squads and platoons deployed for various purposes. Football has a chain of command like the military, starting with the quarterback, who is like a sergeant or

captain, taking part in combat on the field, and going up to the head coach, who is like a general back in headquarters, not directly engaged in battlefield action. Like armies, the teams on the football field defend and attack territory.

3. Football employs warlike generalship. Like a general with his staff, the head coach with his staff of assistants plans strategy and tactics for each game and for the entire campaign. They devise maneuvers to surprise and overwhelm the opponent. They send advance scouts to observe the opposition before the day of combat and study videotapes of the enemy to guard against strengths and discover weaknesses. After the game, they review the performance of their troops to deploy them to best advantage next time.

4. Football employs warlike hand-to-hand combat. Defensive players lay hands on ball carriers to bring them down to earth. As soldiers will sack a town, so defensive linemen will attempt to sack a quarterback by grabbing him and bringing him heavily down to earth before he can divest himself of the ball. A play in football begins with members of the offensive and defensive lines crashing into each other, pushing and shoving with their bodies as in hand-to-hand combat even if not always using their hands. After an especially bruising play, individual members of teams will sometimes start fistfights with the opposition.

Any way you look at it, then, in what the players wear and how they play, football is like war—fortunately without the killing.

Exercise 5.4. Make at least one rearrangement in the order of the paragraphs in the theme of Exercise 5.3 to give it a more logical progression of ideas. Then add Step 5 appropriate for the new arrangement.

6

Step 6: Final Connections

STEP 6: Make sure every sentence is connected to the one before it: by a pronoun, key word or associated word to connect the topic; by a connective word to connect the ideas, or by both.

Step 6 is the final check you apply to your paper to make sure it says what you want to say—and to give it a final professional touch.

On a smaller sentence-to-sentence level, Step 6 applies the same concern for connections that Step 5 makes from paragraph to paragraph. Since the units contained in Step 6 are smaller, the connections can be smaller too. Step 5 requires both the connection of topics (through key words) and the connection of ideas (through connective words). Step 6, on the other hand, will be satisfied if just one kind of connection is made.

In fact, too much connection at the smaller Step 6 level can overwhelm and distract from the development of the paragraph. So Step 6 allows simpler, less noticeable kinds of connection than Step 5.

Step 6 is a natural component of good writing. If <u>a theme</u> has properly kept to the point, its <u>Step 6</u> connections are likely to be in place already. <u>Therefore, Step 6</u> usually will not require much in the way of changes. <u>In fact</u>, you may be pleasantly surprised to find that your theme already has all the <u>Step 6</u> needed. <u>So</u> the instruction for <u>Step 6</u> is not to "change" or "add," but just to "make sure." <u>It</u> is a check on the clarity of what has been written rather than a requirement to add new material.

(The underlined words in the previous paragraph are examples of Step 6. Each connects a sentence to the one before it.)

Like Step 5, Step 6 involves looking backwards. In Step 5, at the start of each new paragraph you look back at the previous paragraph, find key words there, and then insert them along with connective words in the first sentence of the new paragraph. Step 6 does the same thing within each paragraph, sentence by sentence. In each new sentence, look to see if it makes a connection with the sentence before it.

What kind of Step 6 connection do you look for? It can be a connection to a topic in the preceding sentence, using pronouns, key words or associated words; or it can be a connection to the idea of the preceding sentence, using connective words.

(In the marked paragraph, *a theme, Step 6,* and *it* are connections to topics; *Therefore, In fact,* and *So* make connections from one idea to the next.)

A. Connecting Topics

As in Step 5, picking up key words from the previous sentence is one way to link a new sentence to the one before it by topic. But in Step 6 the topic connection may be made with pronouns and other associated words as well.

Here are six ways to do it. In the second of any two sentences:

1. Use a pronoun or other pro-word to refer to someone or something in the previous sentence. (Pronouns include *she, her, hers; he, his, him; it, its; they, their, theirs, them;* and when standing alone rather than modifying another word, *this, that; these, those; some, any, each; another, others; none, all.*) This is the most common Step 6 connection of all. It occurs frequently in the sample themes of this book, as in this case:

> (A) For example, thirteen-year-old Barbara shares her parents' beliefs about the environment. (B) <u>She</u> calls her friend Kiki and says of her neighbors, (C) "Aren't <u>they</u> gross? (D) <u>They</u> don't even recycle their aluminum cans but just put them in the trash. (E) And I heard <u>them</u> laughing about our compost pile. (F) <u>It</u>'s disgusting. . . .

The underlined words are pronouns making Step 6 references to people or things in the immediately preceding sentences. In the sentence labeled (B), *She* at the start of the sentence refers to *Barbara* in Sentence (A). Then in sentence (C), *they* refers to the *neighbors* of the previous sentence. Sometimes a pronoun can refer to another pronoun, as in the case of *They* starting sentence (D) and *them* near the start of sentence (E). Finally, in (F), *It* refers to *laughing* in the immediately preceding sentence.

Here is another example:

> (A) The aldermen let the 30-day period pass without any action. (B) <u>That</u> put the measure on the ballot by default.

In addition to pronouns, *here* and *there* can refer to a place in the previous sentence, *then* to a time, and *do* (*did*, etc.) to a verb and what goes with it—the predicate of a sentence. For example:

> (A) In 1991 I won the lottery. (B) Since *then* my luck has turned sour.

> (A) In 1984 Johnson headed south to enroll in Azusa Pacific University. (B) There he developed his motivating conviction that he could be the best.

> (A) As a 1988 Olympic veteran, the 29-year-old Johnson had battle-tested nerves. (B) O'Brien did not.

2. Repeat a key word or words from the previous sentence. This is what Step 5 requires for paragraph-to-paragraph connections, but it also works for Step 6. Among the many examples of its use from sentence to sentence is the first paragraph of the theme in Exercise 5.3:

> (A) Football employs warlike clothing. (B) The most striking example of warlike clothing is the helmet all players wear. (C) Like a soldier's helmet in war. . . .

In sentence (B), *warlike* and *clothing* are key words (or a key phrase) repeated from sentence (A); in sentence (C), *helmet* is a key word repeated from (B), the sentence immediately before it.

3. Use a synonym, a word or phrase that stands for and means approximately the same as one in the preceding sentence. For example, here is a pair of sentences from the Step 4 theme on studying in Brazil (Exercise 4.11). Sentence (B) uses *The holiday* as a synonym for *Christmas* in the previous sentence.

(A) Since the seasons are the opposite of ours, the temperature is over 110 degrees on Christmas day. (B) The holiday seems strange anyway. . . .

4. Use an antonym. Even a word that means the opposite of one in the previous sentence can be a link in the reader's mind, like *hot* with *cold, night* with *day, concave* with *convex, beautiful* with *ugly*. The relationship between words need not be an exact opposite as long as it is a clear opposition: *round* with *square, parent* with *child, summer* with *winter*. The following example from the theme on football contrasts *after* in (B) with *before* in (A):

(A) They send advance scouts to observe the opposition before the day of combat and study videotapes of the enemy to guard against strengths and discover weaknesses. (B) After the game, they. . . .

5. Use an associated word. We associate *pepper* with *salt, ink* with *pen*, a *pod* with *peas, board* with *room, fork* and *spoon* with *knife, white* and *blue* with *red*, and so on, even though they are neither synonyms nor opposites. Here is an example of *children* associated with *families*:

(A) Families throughout the entire metropolitan area considered a day at Riverview a highlight of the summer season. (B) Children who did not get to go to Riverview at least once a year felt sorely abused.

6. Repeat a sentence structure. This often goes with repeated key words as well:

(A) If I speak in the tongues of men and of angels, but have not love, I am a noisy gong or a clanging cymbal. (B) And if I have prophetic powers, and understand all mysteries and all knowledge; and if I have faith, so as to remove mountains, but have not love, I am nothing. (C) If I give away all I have, and if I deliver my body to be burned, but have not love, I am nothing.

(A) Beyond the opening and between it and the top of the ridge they could see no flames but there was dense smoke. (B) Beyond the opening in the smoke there could be fire—(C) beyond, there could be more reefs, reefs without openings. (D) It could be that beyond the opening was the end of God and the end of youth. [Norman Maclean, *Young Men and Fire*]

B. Connecting Ideas: Connective Words

Connecting topics by one of the six methods just mentioned is a relatively straightforward process. It is simply a matter of finding a pronoun or other word or phrase that will remind the reader of a word or phrase in the preceding sentence. Any such pronoun, word or phrase will do.

More difficult is the second kind of connection, the connection of ideas. Whether from paragraph to paragraph as in Step 5, or from sentence to sentence as in Step 6, connecting ideas requires a choice. Different connective words make different kinds of connections, and only one kind is right in any particular case. So the writer must first determine what kind of connection is being made, and then choose a connective word or phrase that indicates that kind of connection.

The main types of connection are **addition, example, identity, opposite, cause-and-effect,** and **concession**. There is also a special kind of connective we will call **focusing**. Each type has its own collection of connective words.

1. Addition. (Connective words: *and, also, too, additionally, in addition, moreover, likewise, similarly, furthermore, as well as, along with, another, again, besides, in the same way; not only . . . but also; next; first, second, third,* etc.) This is the most frequent kind of connection: one more thing going along with the idea expressed before. In a simple theme, each new paragraph is usually one more thing to explain and support the point, so addition was the one connection explained in the previous chapter for use with Step 5. Addition is an equally fundamental kind of connection on the Step 6 sentence-to-sentence level. For example:

> (A) They don't even recycle their aluminum cans but just put them in the trash. (B) <u>And</u> I heard them laughing about our compost pile.

> (A) Over the years, verandahs and other alterations had obscured the classical appearance of the observatory. (B) <u>Moreover</u>, the building was in deplorable condition.

2. Example. (Connective words: *for example, for instance, as an example, as a sample, to illustrate, such as,* etc.) Giving examples is a frequent way of explaining and supporting a point, and is also one way to fulfill the requirements of Step 4, so example connectives are especially useful. In the paragraph below, sentence (B) begins with a *For example* that indicates it will offer an example to illustrate the point in sentence (A). That example occupies two full sentences, and then (D) begins with *Another example* to indicate the change from the example of the previous sentence to a new one.

> (A) Children imitate their parents' actions. (B) <u>For example</u>, when her mother, a teacher, sat down to grade papers, seven-year-old Agnes brought some sheets of notebook paper and her own red pen to

the table and began scribbling in the margins and writing A's and B's at the top of the pages. (C) When the mother took a break to get a glass of iced tea, the daughter also got up from the table and fixed her own glass with the same ice cubes and squeeze-bottle lemon (but no sugar) as her mother. (D) <u>Another example</u> is. . . .

3. Identity, a restatement of the idea in the previous sentence to explain it more fully. (Connective words: *that is, in other words, to put it another way, to be exact, I mean, in short,* etc.)

(A) The software program uses fuzzy logic. (B) <u>In other words,</u> it allows concepts to be more or less true rather than totally true or totally false.

4. Opposite. (Connective words: *but, yet, however, nevertheless, nonetheless, notwithstanding, still, though, although, on the contrary, whereas, in contrast, rather, instead,* etc.) The second idea does not have to be the strict logical opposite of the first, but merely a contrast or surprise—something different from what would be expected.

(A) From a social point of view, flooding is, of course, a bad thing. (B) <u>But</u> from an environmental point of view, it has certain virtues.

(A) It is sometimes hard to understand fine students. Be sure, <u>though,</u> he had a theory, as fine students nearly always have. [Norman Maclean, *Young Men and Fire*]

5. Cause and effect. (Connective words: *therefore, so, consequently, accordingly, thus, then, as a result, hence, it follows that, because, since,* etc.)

(A) The canal has attracted tourists and that in turn has prompted businesspeople to make improvements. (B) <u>So</u> the whole thing has acted as a kind of catalyst.

(A) Madame Bovary was bored with life in the country. (B) <u>As a result</u>, she left for the city.

6. Concession (presenting the other side). (Connective words: *true, granted, admittedly, of course, naturally, unfortunately, some people say* [or *believe*], *it could be argued that, it is said, it has been falsely claimed, we have been told that*, etc.) This kind of connective is essential in a two-sided theme, one that not only makes a point but considers arguments against it. (See Chapter 9.) In such a theme, the concession connectives are needed in Step 5 to declare when the writer is giving the other side—a view the writer wishes to consider but which is in disagreement with the writer's own point. After giving the other side, the writer signals a return to the original point with the connective *But*. The combination of concessive with *But* can also occur as Step 6 within a paragraph:

(A) She is returning in the 400-m and 800-m freestyle, not having lost at either distance in five years. (B) <u>True,</u> she isn't close to her best times. (C) <u>But</u> neither is anyone else.

7. Focusing. (Connective words: *now, indeed, in fact, well, anyhow*, etc. When *now* is used this way, it does not mean "at this moment in time" but functions as a kind of exclamation.) This is different from the others. With this kind of connective, the tie to the previous idea is less specific than with the previous six types, so it provides less guidance to the reader. What it does is alert the reader that a new point is about to be made.

(A) Barcelona is and always has been a place of industry. (B) <u>In fact</u>, for most of the 19th century it was the only industrial city in Spain.

(A) Like all his friends, my son, age 7, wants to see Batman. (B) I don't allow him to. (C) <u>Now</u>, for the individual father this is no big deal.

This completes the overview of the six ways of connecting topics and seven ways of connecting ideas. One or more of the ways may be observed in each sentence of most well-written paragraphs, including those that follow the first five steps. It might be asked, then, if it is already present, why bother with Step 6? One answer is that it provides a check on how successfully you have accomplished the earlier steps. A more important answer is that it makes you aware of the connections you have established from sentence to sentence, and allows you to change them if you wish.

With this chapter, the basic instruction of this book is complete. All that remains necessary is practice. About half a dozen themes written according to the six steps will be sufficient to put them firmly in mind so that they may be readily recalled in later writing—for they are not an end in themselves but guidelines that can strengthen any writing in the future.

After this chapter, this book turns to more advanced matters. The six steps produce a simple theme, making one straightforward point, but the principles may be applied to more complex writing assignments as well. Some of those additional possibilities, and matters of style, will be the subjects of the remaining chapters.

Assignment 6

In the theme you wrote for Assignments 1 through 5, check every sentence to make sure it has a Step 6 connection with the sentence before it. If there is none, add one. Underline that Step 6 connection.

Exercises

Exercise 6.1. In a published paragraph, <u>underline</u> the Step 6 connections by topic and circle the Step 6 connections made by connective words. If there is more than one Step 6 connection in a sentence, mark only the first. For each, tell what specific kind it is: pronoun, repeated key word, synonym; addition, example, etc. If no Step 6 connection is made in a particular sentence, add an appropriate one.

Exercise 6.2. In one of the sample themes in this book, or in a published piece of writing, find a paragraph whose Step 6 connections are topic connections only. To each sentence in the paragraph (after the first), add a connective word or phrase to connect the ideas. In each case, determine which kind of connection is appropriate—addition, example, etc. Then choose a connective word or phrase of that type. (This exercise does not necessarily improve the paragraph. Generally, having a connective word or phrase in every sentence makes the paragraph too heavy with connectives.)

Exercise 6.3. The following sets of sentences make Step 6 connections to topics in the preceding sentences. In each set, starting with sentence (B), underline the word or words that make the Step 6 connection and circle the word or words in the previous sentence to which the underlined words refer. (If there is more than one Step 6 connection in a sentence, mark only the first.) Then tell what kind of connection is being made—pronoun, key word, etc.

1. (A) The Guess-Your-Weight man tried to lose prizes on the ten-cent game. (B) The prizes there were good public relations.

2. (A) Humans find themselves sexually aroused

by looking at certain arrangements of very small dots on paper or celluloid or magnetic tape. (B) They pay money to look at these patterns. [Carl Sagan and Ann Druyan, *Shadows of Forgotten Ancestors.*]

3. (A) The cashier at my local Waldenbooks has a tacit agreement with me. (B) Whenever I order more copies of my favorite book, neither one of us ever attempts to pronounce the name of the author. (C) The name is Mihaly Csikszentmihalyi, author of *Flow: The Psychology of Optimal Experience.*

4. (A) The tunnel bores still run below the surface of practically all the streets in the Loop. (B) Extensions reach as far south as 16th Street, as far north as Erie Street, and as far west as Halsted Street. (C) Some stretches were destroyed when passenger subways were dug under State, Dearborn, and Lake streets, although the subway does not lie quite as far down as the tunnel. (D) The vast black hole, with its vast possibilities, is now almost universally regarded as a white elephant—a liability rather than an asset.

5. (A) There has been a real revolution in Maya archaeology. (B) It comes from two things. (C) One is the scientific revolution—carbon dating and other geochemical techniques, but especially extensive settlement pattern studies. (D) Archaeologists, beginning with Gordon Willey and others, went out from the centers and mapped the commoners, household by household, plotted the nature of the cities, and having done that, looked at the society from the top to the bottom. (E) That led to a revolution in how

we viewed the Maya. (F) It made us understand that the cities and the populations were much larger than we had thought, the societies more complex, and ecological and agricultural systems more sophisticated than we had realized.

6. (A) It turned out to be a fascinating combination of philosophy, intellectual history, cultural trends, vocabulary enrichment, and applied semantics. (B) All were strikingly mingled. (C) Participation in discussion was strongly encouraged. (D) Intellectual curiosity was boldly stimulated. (E) Spontaneous communication was vibrantly unleashed.

Exercise 6.4. The following sets of sentences use connective words to make Step 6 connections to ideas in the preceding sentences. In each set, starting with sentence (B), underline the word or words that make the Step 6 connection. Then tell what kind of connection is being made—addition, example, identity, etc.

1. (A) Well, see, this here is a topless bar. (B) And back home I introduced legislation to close down topless bars. (C) So you can see that this wouldn't look too good.

2. (A) Although I have had few school courses in science, I have always tried hard to be accurate with facts. (B) In addition, I found that being accurate with facts was a kind of game and I liked to play it. (C) Later, when I came to know some great scientists, I found that to them science was a kind of game on a grand scale. [Norman Maclean, *Young Men and Fire*]

Exercise 6.5. 1. In the proper place in the following pair of sentences, add a Step 6 connective word or phrase to show a cause-and-effect relationship.

(A) The weather is cold. (B) The windows of the classroom are closed.

2. In the proper place in the following pair of sentences, add a Step 6 connective word or phrase to show an *opposite* relationship.

(A) It is the holiday season. (B) Students are taking final exams.

3. In the proper place in the following pair of sentences, add a Step 6 connective word or phrase to show a cause-and-effect relationship.

(A) It is the holiday season. (B) Students are taking final exams.

Exercise 6.6. Connective words tell the reader what kind of connection to make between two sentences. What kind of connection is made between each of the following pairs? What is the difference in meaning between 1 and 2?

1. (A) Business was fine. (B) So the manager closed the store early.

2. (A) Business was fine. (B) But the manager closed the store early.

Exercise 6.7. For each of the following pairs of sentences, decide which type of connective—addition, example, identity, opposite, or cause and effect—is most appropriate and then insert in the second sentence a connective word of that type.

1. (A) Last night I couldn't sleep. (B) Today I can't stay awake.

2. (A) Sam got an F in American history. (B) He doesn't care.

3. (A) Judy got an F in American history. (B) She didn't study.

4. (A) Judy got an A in American history. (B) She didn't study.

5. (A) Jim got an A in all his classes. (B) He's on the Dean's List this semester.

6. (A) I got a C in American history. (B) I got an A in chemistry.

7. (A) Gretchen followed Steps 1, 2, and 3. (B) She used many excellent details.

Exercise 6.8. Turn to the theme on football in Exercise 5.3. In each paragraph, underline the Step 6 connections at the start of sentences, and tell what types of connections they make.

Exercise 6.9. Find all the Step 6 connections in Lincoln's Gettysburg Address. (For this exercise, consider it one single paragraph.) Tell whether each is a topic or idea connection, and what specific kind it is: repeated key word, pronoun, synonym or antonym, addition, example, etc. Note how many such connections Lincoln uses within his sentences (though those do not count as Step 6), as well as from sentence to sentence.

Chapter
7

Style

The way something is written should reflect its meaning: form should follow function.

Do not hesitate to repeat key words.

Keep to the same grammatical subject.

Achieve variety not by changing vocabulary but by making every third sentence or so noticeably longer than the others, and starting every third sentence or so with something other than the grammatical subject.

Even in a book that focuses on the expression of ideas, it is appropriate to mention a few principles of style that will enhance that expression.

Style is the dress or clothing of writing. Like clothing, it is important in creating the right impression, but it has little to do with the actual health, character, and intelligence of the person who wears it.

In writing, a person who uses words smoothly and eloquently will have a stylistic advantage over someone whose writing is more rough and plain. But that does not mean the smooth talker will necessarily get the job done any better. If the goal of writing is to communicate a point, as in real life it usually is, then those who have a point to make (Step 1), stick to it (Steps 2 and 3), support it in detail (Step 4), and guide the reader through the explanation (Steps 5 and 6) will reach that goal, whether their writing happens to be ornamented or plain. A team with neatly pressed, fancy uniforms does not necessarily defeat one with uniforms that are plain and perhaps in need of cleaning. In fact, too much attention to the uniforms instead of the game may detract from success on the field.

So this book on the principles of writing to the point does not dwell on the myriad of details that make for an impressive style. There are many handbooks that discuss those details. But there are a few basic principles of style that are simple to follow and that can make a significant difference in the impact of one's writing, because, like the six steps, they help clarify the point and present it in an orderly fashion.

Amid the thousands of stylistic details, these few principles are easy to overlook. Here we will mention these principles only, leaving the other matters of style to the kind of books mentioned above.

A. Form Follows Function

The most fundamental principle of style is that the way something is said should reflect what is being said— that is, form should follow function.

The method of writing taught by the six steps follows this principle. Most important in a communication is the point to be communicated, so the point is stated at the most emphatic places in a theme, at the beginning (Step 1) and at the end (the rounding-off sentence).

Next most important are the main subpoints (Step 2), so those have the second most important places of emphasis, the beginnings of each of the paragraphs. The details that support the point are assigned to the most detailed sentences (Steps 3 and 4). The larger connections between paragraphs require more in the way of connecting words (Step 5) than do the smaller connections between sentences (Step 6).

The principle that form follows function applies in other ways, too. On a larger scale, it means that important matters should have more space and attention than less important matters. The most important Step 2 reason or example should go in an emphatic place, in the first or last paragraph rather than in the middle. Likewise, the most important and convincing Step 4 example should have the most prominent place and the lengthiest, most detailed explanation.

Even within a single sentence, form should follow function. If there are several equal items, for example, they should be treated equally, in parallel form: *She likes squash soup, spinach salad, and twice-baked potatoes* rather than **She likes squash soup, not to mention spinach salad, twice-baked potatoes being yet another of her favorites.* In the starred version, the changes in position and connectives confuse the reader and obscure the simple message that there are three foods she likes.

Likewise, when there are matters with different degrees of importance, that difference should show in the form. The main points should occupy the major parts of sentences, while less important points should occupy the minor parts. Consider a statement like this: *Returning from rescuing a family of five from the flood, my neighbor tracked muddy footprints onto the formerly clean kitchen floor—eight footprints heading for the sink and getting gradually fainter.* Devoting twice as many words to the kitchen floor as to the rescue suggests that the floor is twice as important.

It is not only the number of words but their role in the sentence that can make a difference in emphasis. The difference between *but* and *though* illustrates this. Both are connective words that signal the opposite of what one might expect from what has come before. The difference is that what follows *but* is a main clause or main point, and what follows *though* is a subordinate clause or subordinate point. What follows *though* is (at least grammatically) not as important as the main statement of the sentence. In *I decided to go, but it was raining,* the most important factor is the rain, and the message is that the writer did not go. In contrast, in the sentence *I decided to go, though it was raining,* the statement about rain is subordinate, not the main point, and we understand the main point to be that the writer did go.

B. Repetition

Some would-be writers believe there is a commandment not to repeat key words, no matter what the cost. At the cost of clarity, or parallel expression of ideas, they will change words as often as possible, sometimes with the help of a thesaurus. This must be done, they believe, to avoid monotony and achieve a variety that will keep the reader's interest.

But it does not. That way of achieving variety makes about as much sense as requiring actors in a play to change costumes every time they exit and enter in order to keep the attention of the audience. And it is just as harmful to the point. That is because there are no exact synonyms. Two words may refer to the same person or thing, but they do so from different perspectives. If you change a word, you are changing the meaning.

So if I first write about *this book* and then, to avoid repeating *book*, refer to *this pamphlet*, my new word makes you think of its smallness. If I call it *this volume*, you think of how thick it is. And it becomes even thicker and weightier if I fish in my thesaurus to come up with *this tome*.

Lincoln would not have held his audience if he had ended the Gettysburg Address with "government of the people, by the populace, for the population." The audience would lose track of the main point wondering what the differences were: How is *populace* different from *people*? Is *population* something else again?

One of the important differences between professional and amateur writing is that professionals freely repeat key words and use parallel statements for parallel ideas. They welcome repetition to make their ideas clear and keep the focus and emphasis on their main points.

C. Consistent Grammatical Subject

The mistaken impulse to change for variety's sake shows up especially when dealing with indefinite or hypothetical subjects: a student, a voter, a contestant, a writer, a scientist, and so on. It is possible to think of *a student* or of *students*, of *her* or of *him*, to address *you* or write about *us*—but it is distracting to the reader to switch from one to the other. Choose one way of referring to an indefinite subject and then stick to it. This is the wrong way to go about it:

> *Students do his or her worst writing in writing classes. There is something about a writing class that brings out your worst effort. Maybe

we have just too many rules to remember, preventing a student from concentrating on any of them. Thank goodness this chapter has only four rules for us to learn!

The reader of this paragraph wonders why it changes grammatical subjects so often, and in wondering the reader loses sight of the point. Here are two possible ways to change the paragraph to make it consistent:

Students do their worst writing in writing classes. There is something about these classes that brings out their worst effort. Maybe they have just too many rules to remember, preventing students from concentrating on any of them. Thank goodness this chapter has only four rules for students to learn!

or:

We do our worst writing in a writing class. There is something about that class that brings out our worst effort. Maybe we have just too many rules to remember, preventing us from concentrating on any of them. Thank goodness this chapter has only four rules for us to learn!

The first of these changed paragraphs now is clearly more formal; the second is clearly more direct and intimate. Both have also removed the inconsistency of referring first to *classes* (plural) and then to *a class* (singular).

It should be noted also that a paragraph of indefinite reference violates Step 4. That step calls for paragraphs to be as specific as possible and to use examples: not *a student* but *Gretchen Stauder, a senior majoring in fiction writing*. Follow Step 4, being as specific as possible in examples and details, and there will be no trouble keeping the subject consistent.

D. Variety

Professionals achieve variety not by changing vocabulary but by changing the length and type of sentences—especially the Step 4 sentences that give the detailed evidence in support of their points. Just as there will be great variety in details, so the sentences that give the details can be varied. Here are two simple stylistic rules to ensure that sentences have variety:

1. Make every third sentence or so noticeably longer than the others.

2. Start every third sentence or so with something other than the grammatical subject. (The subject is *who* or *what* is or does. Simple sentences such as those specified for Steps 1 and 2 usually begin with the subject. But within a paragraph it is possible to put something else in front of the subject—a connective word or words, for example, or a word or phrase indicating place or time, or even a whole subordinate clause.)

Here is an example of a monotonous paragraph that does not follow these rules:

*(A) I was also beginning to feel how enormous and varied Denali is. (B) The ranger station for the southern portion lies outside the park in Talkeetna. (C) Few people hike into this rugged side of Denali. (D) Talkeetna's flying services nevertheless handle an increasing number of sightseers. (E) The majority of McKinley climbers fly to base camps from her as well. (F) The sleepy, winterbound village thaws to become a hive of summit-struck folk.

The six sentences are all similar in length, from 10 to 14 words, and all begin with their grammatical subject.

Now consider the same paragraph revised, as it actually appeared in *National Geographic*:

(A) I was also beginning to feel how enormous and varied Denali is. (B) The ranger station for the southern portion lies outside the park in Talkeetna. (C, D) *Although* few hike into this rugged side of Denali, Talkeetna's flying services handle an increasing number of sightseers. (E, F) The majority of McKinley climbers fly to base camps from here as well; the sleepy, winterbound village thaws to become a hive of slightly wild-eyed, summit-struck folk spouting foreign languages.

For variety in length, sentences C and D are now combined to make a sentence of 18 words, and E and F make a noticeably longer combination of 32. The new combined sentence C, D no longer begins with the grammatical subject but with *Although* introducing a subordinate clause.

In both of these rules, "or so" indicates needed flexibility. If exactly every third sentence were exactly twice as long as the others, and if exactly every third sentence began with a place, or a time, or a subordinate clause, the effect would be even more monotonous than the monotony the rules are designed to avoid. Let the variety and complexity of the details govern the form of the writing, but check to make sure every third sentence or so ends up with a different shape.

Assignment 7

In the themes you have previously written, check to see that the grammatical subjects are consistent. Then look at each paragraph and rewrite as necessary to make every third sentence or so noticeably longer than the others, and every third sentence or so begin with something other than the grammatical subject. Perform this check on your writing in the future as well.

Review Assignment

With all six steps now presented, along with the rules of style, it is time for review and practice. Before going on to the refinements in Chapters 8 through 10, write at least three more themes following all six steps and the Chapter 7 rules of style. Use Step 1 and Step 2 sentences generated in the exercises of Chapters 1 and 2, or write about a person you know, a place you know, a mode of transportation, a meal, a holiday, or a season. Double space and follow the format shown in the previous chapters.

Exercises

Exercise 7.1. Make the subject consistent in the following paragraph. Change only those words necessary to accomplish this.

> A student who is not wealthy ought to find a college with low costs. In fact, if students sat down and figured all the expenses before they enrolled in college, he or she might avoid serious trouble. An expensive school is not necessarily a good school. Actually, what college gives you depends mostly on how seriously you do your work there, whether attending it is expensive or not. If we loaf through school, no amount of money paid is going to make much out of us.

Exercise 7.2. Rewrite the paragraph about writing classes so that its subject is *a student*. (You can also use *he or she, she or he*.) Avoid the plural *students* and *they*, and avoid the first or second person *I, we, you*.

8

Comparison and Contrast

In a contrast theme:

1. Make a specific Step 1 statement. Do not just say that two objects or persons are different; say what the basic difference is.

2. Select significant differences, not trivial ones.

3. Include only material that relates to the contrast.

4. If you mention something about one object or person, mention the same thing about the other.

5. Take up things in the order in which you first present them.

6. Indicate contrasts with connective words that signal opposite ideas.

The most sophisticated writing, as well as the most simple, uses the principles embodied in the six steps. Now it is time to consider one of the more sophisticated forms: contrast.

Looking at two people or things side by side sharpens our understanding of both. Two presidents, two roommates, two restaurants, two books: each takes on clearer definition when considered against the background of the other. But keeping two (or more) subjects always in mind, rather than just one, also makes the task of writing more complex, and so our previous explanation of the six steps has avoided contrast. Now it is time to incorporate that valuable activity.

The basis of contrast is comparison: putting two or more objects side by side and considering each from the same perspectives. To contrast is to focus on the differences we find. But differences are usually important only if there are important similarities, too. We find it more useful to contrast one tennis player with another than to contrast a tennis player with a golfer. We find it more useful to contrast two politicians running for the same political office than to contrast those running for different offices. Similarly, we usually do not find it very useful to contrast a politician with a tennis pro, because the major differences are so obvious that they tell us little about the particular individuals.

Once you have found a suitable pair for contrast, here is what to do with it.

1. Make a specific Step 1 statement. Do not just say that two objects or persons are different; say what the basic difference is.

It is not enough in Step 1 to say *College is different from high school* or *College is like high school*. That is as useful as saying *College is the subject matter of this theme*. No, any two people or objects have countless differences and similarities. The question is, which difference is basic?

Perhaps your view is that *College is more demanding than high school* or that *College puts more responsibility on the student than high school* or *College allows students more independence than high school*—or perhaps, in your experience, *College is easier than high school.* Any of these points would provide a sharp Step 1 focus for developing a theme.

2. Select significant differences, not trivial ones.

There are thousands of ways to contrast any two objects or individuals. The question is, which ways really make a difference? Which ones are significant?

Consider college and high school again. In college, the instructors are called professors; in high school, they are called teachers. At a college, the chief administrator is usually a president or chancellor; at a high school, the chief is called a principal. Are these the most significant differences? Probably not, unless you are making a point about the different attitudes of those who work at colleges and high schools.

Not all differences will do. Look for those that provide significant support for, and explanation of, the point.

3. Include only material that relates to the contrast.

If contrast is the business of a theme, stick to business—in every sentence. To put it negatively: nothing that does not get contrasted belongs in the theme. If you are comparing college and high school, and mention the physics lab in college, then you must mention the physics lab (or its equivalent) in high school. If you are comparing the authors Alice Walker and Toni Morrison, and consider it important to tell where and when Walker was born, you must give that information for Morrison as well.

4. If you mention something about one object or person, mention the contrasting thing about the other.

For a fair contrast, the yardstick of measurement cannot change. It is not enough just to say one thing about one and a different thing about the other; the differences must be truly comparable.

To say that apples differ from oranges, because apples are red while oranges are citrus fruit, is not to make a true contrast at all. What color are oranges? What kind of fruit are apples? To say that candidate A deserves election over candidate B, because A keeps promises and B accepts bribes, is not to make a true contrast either. How well does B keep promises? Does A refuse bribes?

5. Take up things in the order in which you first present them.

A contrast involves first a statement about one thing, then a statement about another. With two subjects to keep in mind, the reader has a more difficult task than with a simple theme that involves only one subject and no contrasts. The writer, listing point after point of contrast in Steps 2, 3, and 4, may find it monotonous to present the objects always in the same order. But the reader needs that regularity in order to avoid being confused.

So if you are contrasting college with high school and state in Step 1 that *College offers a wider range of academic choices than high school*, all other sentences in the theme should follow that order: college first, high school second. If Step 1 says *Alice Walker is a more versatile writer than Toni Morrison*, in each of the following comparisons Walker should come first, Morrison second. If an exception is to be made to this rule, save it for the rounding-off sentence at the end, where a twist in the usual order can signify an end to the discussion.

6. Indicate contrasts with connective words that signal opposite ideas.

Another necessity for avoiding confusion in a contrast theme is to use appropriate connective words: those that indicate one item is the opposite of another. Words of this type are listed in section B 4 of Step 6: *but, yet, however,* etc.

Especially useful for a contrast made within a single sentence are whereas and while. The connective is placed between the two halves of the contrast, following a comma:

Oranges are sweet, *whereas* lemons are sour.

Oranges are sweet, *while* lemons are sour.

When the contrast involves two separate sentences, an especially useful connective is the phrase *In contrast*. The second sentence starts with *In contrast* followed by a comma:

Oranges are sweet. *In contrast,* lemons are sour.

The connectives *whereas, while,* and *In contrast* may be used as often as necessary.

X123 in Contrast

The outline of a contrast theme is like that of any other, except that it has two subjects instead of one. So Steps 1 and 2 will look like this:

X College classes are harder than high school classes.

1. Reading assignments are harder in college than in high school.

2. Classes meet less often in college than in high school.

3. Exams are harder in college than in high school.

Each paragraph then goes into detail (Steps 3 and 4) on its particular aspect of the contrast. That's all there is to it, as long as you keep the rules for contrast in mind as you develop the paragraphs. The six steps still apply, but you're juggling two balls in the air instead of one.

And with that, the lesson on contrast comes to an end. But since the ultimate goal of this book is to prepare you for the real writing you will do in the rest of your life (see Chapter 10), here is a glimpse of another way to develop a contrast, one that follows most of the steps but violates Step 2. You would use this when a point-by-point contrast, following Step 2, is not possible. This would be the case, for example, when you are contrasting the personalities or the lives of two people who have led quite different lives. To say that one is more courageous than the other, or more charming, or has led a more exciting life, might not work in the X123 arrangement shown above if the Step 4 detail does not match up point by point. For this situation it would be best to have two Step 2 paragraphs rather than three:

X A is more __ than B.
1. A is __ .
2. B is __ .

You would use this pattern if the individual details of A and B are not directly comparable. The comparison would take place from one paragraph to the next, instead of within each paragraph. This pattern would suit a statement such as *Ronald Reagan was a more influential president than George W. Bush.*

That's enough for that digression. Now back to the usual six steps for the assignments and exercise.

Assignments

Assignment 8.1. Write a theme contrasting college with high school. Follow the six rules of this chapter as well as the six steps. Double space and use the format taught in Chapters 3 and 4.

Assignment 8.2. Contrast two people you know, or two places, two jobs, two types of transportation, two meals, two publications, two college courses, two seasons, men and women, or youth and age. Follow the six rules of this chapter as well as the six steps. Double space and use the format taught in Chapters 3 and 4.

Exercise

Exercise 8.1. The following paragraph from a theme violates one of the rules for contrast. Cross out the place where it breaks the rule and change it just enough to correct the violation.

> Winter is more comfortable than summer. Winter fires in the fireplace are more comfortable than barbecue fires in the summer. Also, the humidity of summer makes it less comfortable than the dry air of winter.

Chapter 9

Argumentation: The Other Side

**To consider two sides of an issue, conclude
your theme with a paragraph that presents
the best argument for the other side, followed
by a paragraph that replies to that argument.
Finish as usual with a rounding-off sentence
that restates your point.**

Before this chapter, your assignments have been like
the drills a team practices to get ready for competition.
Now we move closer to playing the game.

A simple six-step theme is one-sided. It makes one
point and supports it. It is like a case made by a lawyer in court; there may well be another side (with any
interesting statement there usually is), but the simple
theme allows just one point of view. It is a deliberate
simplification in order to present a position as clearly as
possible and to make clear the support for it.

To be sure, presenting only one side can be a sophisticated matter, as anyone who has watched a skilled
lawyer knows. But now it is time to increase the sophis-
tication by adapting the six steps so that the reader,

like the judge and the jury, hears both sides.

Is it indeed possible to adapt the six steps to allow both sides to be heard in a single theme? Yes. This chapter shows how.

Take the simple point that *Children imitate their parents*, for example. It is not hard to find evidence to support this, as shown by the sample theme in Chapters 3 and 4; but anyone looking at the behavior of children would also find evidence of children doing the opposite. There are unathletic children of athletic parents, rude children of polite parents, artistic children of unartistic parents. Evidence is plentiful to support the point that *Children reject their parents' example*. This could be a separate theme. And, according to the six steps as we have presented them thus far, a separate theme would be the only way to consider this opposite view.

But just as some accommodations can be made in the six steps to allow the very useful device of contrast, so it is possible to make some simple adjustments to allow argumentation on both sides of an issue.

There are good reasons to allow both sides in a theme. One reason is to make a more convincing case for the side you favor. A second is to increase the likelihood that you will arrive at the truth. If the evidence persuades you to change your mind, change it.

Presenting the Other Side

To allow the other side will require a variance in Step 2, which specifies that all paragraphs should support the point. We must now have one paragraph near the end of the theme which expresses the best argument against the point, followed by a paragraph replying to it and returning to the point.

In presenting the other side, it is tempting to give a weak argument, the so-called straw man. But to present only a weak argument for the other side is worse than not considering it at all; it suggests that the writer doubts that the main point can withstand serious opposition. No, the persuasiveness of an argumentative theme depends on how well the case is made for the other side—and then how well the writer responds to that case.

Connectives: Concession and Reply

In a theme of this sort, presenting more than one side, Step 5 needs special attention. At all times the writer must make clear 1) which side is being discussed and 2) which side is the main point and which the other side. The connective words under the heading *Concession* in Chapter 6, section B 6, signal the beginning of the other side: *True, granted, admittedly, of course, naturally, unfortunately; some people say, it could be argued that, it is said, it has been falsely claimed, it appears that,* etc. Further connective words throughout the paragraph remind the reader that you are continuing to present the opposing view: *They also say, It could be further argued that,* etc.

When the paragraph of the other side is finished and a new paragraph replying to the other side begins, the word *But* at the start of the new paragraph signals the change. *But* indicates that what follows is the opposite of the previous paragraph, and being the opposite, it returns to the main point.

Here is how a paragraph giving the other side of *Children imitate their parents* might look, followed by a paragraph of reply.

4. [Objection, presenting other side] Admittedly, children do not always copy their parents.

This is especially true of teenagers, who can make a point of rebelling as they establish their own identity. For example, 16-year-old Alex will walk two miles to a friend's house rather than drive or ride in his parents' Volvo station wagon. For another example, when 15-year-old Leah shops for clothes with her mother, she will refuse even to try on anything her mother thinks is attractive. Then there is Cara, 13, whose parents go on a one-mile walk to the rose garden in the park five nights a week. Every time they go, her mother or father will invite her along, saying that it's good exercise and furthermore, they would enjoy her company; she always declines, shuddering at the thought that her friends might see her doing what old people do.

5. [Reply to other side, returning to original point] But though there are clearly some instances where children pointedly avoid imitating their parents, the instances where they do imitate them, even unconsciously, are more common. Alex is more like his father than he may think. When Alex has lost his way, he refuses to ask for directions, just like his father. Leah, for another example, may refuse her mother's advice, but she has her mother's coloring and size, and she often borrows her mother's clothes and jewelry to wear. And Cara likes to go to the very same park her parents do and admire the same rose garden— when her parents aren't there.

[Original rounding-off sentence] So whether it is actions, words, or beliefs, in many ways children imitate their parents.

In the above excerpt, the reply focuses directly on the

other side's examples. While not denying their truth, it counters them with other examples about the same people. (That is because they are true. When the other side's reasoning or evidence is wrong, the reply will say so and explain why it is wrong.) One way or another, the paragraph immediately after the statement of the other side must directly reply to it and bring the reader back to the main point.

X123 with the Other Side

Where do these two paragraphs fit in? Generally they go best at the end of the theme, after you have made and explained your point. (Sometimes a writer begins with the other side and spends the rest of the essay replying to it. Thomas Aquinas, a famous medieval churchman, organized his *Summa Theologica* that way. You can try it too, once you have mastered this simpler arrangement.)

You can add the objection and reply to a theme as the fourth and fifth paragraphs, as in the additions to the *Children imitate their parents* theme:

X [Main point]
1. [First supporting point]
2. [Second supporting point]
3. [Third supporting point]
4. [Objection to point]
5. [Reply to objection, supporting the main point again]

Or, since a theme needs only three paragraphs, you can cut to the chase, making the objection and reply the second and third paragraphs:

X [Main point]
1. [Supporting point]
2. [Objection to point]
3. [Reply to objection, supporting the main point again]

What if the other side turns out to be so persuasive that you, the writer, are persuaded by it? In that case, switch sides. Go for the truth. Revise your Step 1 and 2 sentences and rearrange your paragraphs, so that the former other side is now the main point, and the former main point is now the other side.

And what if, after weighing the evidence on both sides, you cannot make up your mind? Well, you could venture a Step 1 sentence like *There is good evidence on both sides of the question of —*. But please don't. Your job as a writer is to inform your reader; that means sifting through the evidence and taking a stand. Do your reader the service of stating the conclusion that the best evidence leads to, even as you face up to the strongest objection to that conclusion.

Assignment 9

Write an argumentative theme that includes a statement of the best argument for the other side, followed by a direct reply to that statement. Use the proper connective words to indicate the other side and the return to your own position. Place the statement of the other side at the most logical and effective point.

For one possible topic, write about a decision you have made where you have seriously considered the other side. The Step 1 sentence will be the choice you made: College A was a good choice for me, Job B suits my abilities, It was time to end my relationship with C.

Exercises

Exercise 9.1. In a published piece of writing that argues a point, such as a newspaper editorial or opinion column, tell what the writer's main point is and then underline all statements that consider the other side. Circle the concessive connective words that let the reader know this is the other side.

Exercise 9.2. To the sample theme on football in Exercise 5.3, add a paragraph expressing the other side and then a paragraph replying to it. Tell where you would locate those new paragraphs, and tell the Step 5 changes you would make as a result.

Exercise 9.3. To any of the themes you have previously written, add a paragraph expressing the other side and then a paragraph replying to it. Tell where you would locate those new paragraphs, and tell the Step 5 changes you would make as a result.

Exercise 9.4. Do the same as in Exercise 9.3 for the contrast theme of Assignment 8. Continue to follow the rules of contrast as you incorporate the other side and a reply to it. This exercise will require careful planning and execution.

Chapter

10

The Real World

In all of your writing, follow each of the six steps, or have a reason for not doing so.

The principles of writing to the point, as explained in the previous nine chapters, are principles that apply to all kinds of writing. Admittedly, themes exactly like those produced by the six steps are rarely to be found outside of this book. But the claim of this book is that its principles are intended for real writing—writing done not just as a class exercise but in the course of one's actual work or personal life. (Notice the use of connectives, following our principles, in the past three sentences—an example of real-life writing.)

What does X123 have to do with an actual report, letter, or novel? This chapter will explain.

Each of the six steps is useful to a writer. There will be occasions when a writer will not want to follow a particular step, but it should be for a good reason. Here are reasons for following the six steps in real-life writing, and also some reasons to do otherwise for particular purposes.

Step 1: A Starting Point and an Introduction

Making a point (Step 1) is actually more of a common practice in the real world than in a writing class. Outside of class, people usually take the trouble to write only when they have points to make, messages to convey—to inform, persuade, or entertain others. A newspaper story, a job application, a list of regulations, a legal brief, a scientific paper, an advertisement—all have a point to make. People say something because they have something to say.

In a writing class, on the other hand, the reason for writing is to practice writing, so it is easier to neglect making a point. Without a point, thoughts can be random in a way that would not pass in the real world. It is like testing a public address system; asked to "say something" rather than to make a point, people who ordinarily have much to say can think only of "Testing, 1, 2, 3."

Try to get away with that in real life! Walk up to a friend and make a point of speaking pointlessly: "Beverages. Plastic containers. Vitamins A and C. Evaporation. Digestion. Thirst. Black, white, pale yellow, orange, purple, pink, translucent. Baths. Remedies. Prohibition." (Huh?)

If a writing class uses this book, of course, the message is different. Here we insist that all writing be as pointed as it is in the real world: not just random comments on beverages, for example, but some point about them, so that a friend does not have to ask, "Why are you saying this? What's your point?"

There is one major kind of real-life writing that does not always make a point: the narrative. This kind of writing is organized as a story. It tells what happened first, then next, and so on. An anecdote, a fable, a novel, a history, a biography may simply tell what happened, one thing after the next. But even within a narrative there are often points to be made, sometimes stated by the writer, sometimes just implied. There must be some significance, some point at least suggested by the narrative, or the reader is likely to ask, "So what? Why bother telling this story?"

In a simple six-step theme the point is placed prominently by itself at beginning (Step 1) and end (rounding-off sentence). Real life, on the other hand, may call for an introduction before presenting the Step 1 point, and a full paragraph of conclusion to go with the rounding-off sentence. But introductions and conclusions are not required with all real-life writing, either. The question is not, "What should I say for an introduction?" but "Do I need one? Would it help or annoy the reader?"

In real-life writing there is often as little need for an introduction as there is when you are talking with friends, family, or employer. A report to shareholders does not have to begin with the statement, "Profits are important to business"; a text message to a parent does not need to start with "Children's activities are always of interest to their parents."

An introduction can insult the reader by stating the obvious, as if the reader doesn't know it already; or by misleading the reader into thinking you're going to write about something else. Only if you have a good reason—to establish your credentials, or give background on an unfamiliar topic, or explain why a reader should care about your subject matter—should you bother with an introduction.

Step 2: Paragraphs

In support of the main point, Step 2 assigns each major subpoint to the start of a new paragraph. That follows an elementary principle of organization: a new paragraph for each new idea.

Real-life paragraphs follow this principle, too. A new paragraph announces the end of one subpoint and the beginning of another. The reader understands that a new line and an indentation mean more of a break than just a period and a space.

However, real-life writing often introduces new paragraphs more frequently than Step 2 would require. New paragraphs come at major subpoints, just as specified by Step 2. But in real-life writing they also come at minor ones, for each new example or detail.

In newspaper stories, for example, very little progression of thought often is a new paragraph—like this.

Changing paragraphs with each little change in thought may help the reader follow the writer's line of thinking. It also gives the reader more places to pause. In many instances, little paragraphs are user-friendly.

But to change paragraphs at every minor point runs the risk of obscuring the major changes from one Step 2 statement to another. Step 5, which signals those changes, is even more important when paragraphs are broken into small pieces.

Step 3 and Digression

The underlying purpose of Step 3 is to remind the writer to keep to the point rather than drift to some other interesting matter.

This principle considers the time limits and attention span of the reader. All of us know the boredom that results when someone cannot keep to the point: "The funniest thing happened to me today! I was walking down

28th Street—or was it 29th Street? Let's see, there's a convenience store on the corner of 28th and State. No, it moved. And in such a short time! I remember when it opened just a year ago. Or was it two years ago? Let me see, that was just after I had come back from visiting Aunt Elaine, you know, the one who builds model bridges with toothpicks. . . ."

Examples like this show the value not only of having a point but of keeping to it all the way through, in real-life writing as well as in the six-step theme. But there will be a legitimate exception when something is mentioned that the reader would not understand. Then a sentence or two of background explanation is in order, as in this case for someone who has not heard of bungee jumping: "Bungee jumping can be frightening. (That's when you attach elastic cords to your feet and jump headfirst off a high platform until you almost hit the ground.) The free fall stimulates the most basic fear of falling. . . ."

Step 4: The Facts

If there is any step so fundamental that it applies to almost any kind of writing in real and private life, it is Step 4. Even a story that has no Step 1 point to make needs Step 4.

The importance of Step 4 is that it enables the point, or the story, to be both clear and convincing. To say that *Children imitate their parents* and then explain only that *Children do what their parents do* and *It is amazing how children follow in their parents' footsteps* does not make clear to the reader exactly what kind of imitation is meant, nor does it offer any evidence to persuade the unconvinced reader. But with Step 4 providing specific, concrete detail, the writer gives the reader a picture: something to see, hear, smell, touch, taste. Properly done—when the sentences of each paragraph are as detailed, specific and as concrete as possible—Step 4 gives the reader a sense of being there, of experiencing first hand. If there is one characteristic great writers share, it is the ability to present a scene in specific, concrete detail.

Step 4 is convincing too because it faces the facts. It *is* the facts. All too often writers prefer abstract generalities because they are too lazy or too stubborn to consider the evidence. A refusal to back up a point with real-life evidence is a sign of denying reality.

Step 5: Major Connections

In real-life writing, Step 5 is, if anything, even more helpful than it is in a six-step theme. That is because, as mentioned above, real-life paragraphs cannot be relied on to indicate major changes of thought, as they do in a six-step theme. In real life, often only Step 5 is able to signal when one major point is finished and another begins. So making Step 5 connections between major ideas with key words and connective words is especially important for keeping the point clear in the reader's mind.

Step 6: Connections Everywhere

In any paragraph, every sentence should clearly connect to the sentence before it by topic or idea, or by both. The connections form a chain that helps the reader follow from one sentence to the next. If the chain is broken, the reader is likely to fall off the train of thought. Only if you deliberately want to puzzle or frustrate the reader should you dispense with helpful Step 6.

Longer Writing

The principles of Steps 1 through 6 are not just for short themes. They apply equally well to long papers and to books. A longer theme, instead of having just three or four Step 2 subpoints, might have twice as many, or even more, like this:

X [Main point of theme]
1. [First subpoint]
2. [Second subpoint]
3. [Third subpoint]
4. [Fourth subpoint]
5. [Fifth subpoint]
6. [Sixth subpoint]
[etc.]

A longer theme could also subdivide the Step 2 subpoints further. For a book or long paper, the Step 2 sentences could be the main sections; Step 2A sentences could be chapters, and Step 2B sentences could be main points within chapters—each followed then by the Steps 3 and 4 details in the paragraphs. The outline then might look like this:

X [Main point of book]

   1. [Overall point of first section of book]

      1A. [Overall point of first chapter]

         1B. [First point of first chapter]

         2B. [Second point of first chapter]

         3B. [Third point of first chapter]

         4B. [Fourth point of first chapter]

      2A. [Overall point of second chapter]

   [etc.]

Reading for the Point

The principles of writing embodied in the six steps may be applied in reverse to help with the reading you do. Some of the exercises of the previous chapters have already done this for particular steps. Now we can put the six steps together to provide a systematic approach to reading. They must be applied backward to unravel the details of the writing until we get to the main point, the author's Step 1.

For it is the case that almost every kind of writing, except some fiction, has a point to make, a message to convey. What is it?

To find out, first we look at the connections the author has made (Steps 5 and 6). Pay attention especially to the connection of ideas by connective words. What does it mean when the writer says *In addition, furthermore, that is*? (See Chapter 6, part B.) What is happening when we read *Some people claim* . . . followed by *But*? (See Chapter 9.) Paying close attention to these connective words will make clear which side the author is on, which evidence the author wants us to believe, and which evidence the author wants us to doubt.

That brings us back to Steps 3 and 4, the presentation of the evidence. What evidence does the author provide? How detailed, specific, and concrete is it? (Step 4.) And what does the author devote the most space to? As Chapter 7 has explained, matters that take up the greatest amount of space usually have the greatest importance for the writer.

Having recognized the connections and the evidence, we now look for the main subpoints, the Step 2 statements. They do not always come at the start of paragraphs as in a simple theme; we have to look for them throughout the paragraphs, sometimes even at the end. And we have to remember that, in writing that has many short paragraphs, not every paragraph has a main point. But guided by Step 5, and looking for statements that make points about the various pieces of evidence, we can find whatever subpoints there are.

Finally, recognizing the subpoints, we look for a statement that sums them up, a sentence that accounts for all of the subpoints and evidence (Step 1). This statement is often found in emphatic places (at the beginning and end), and good writers often repeat it to give it emphasis and make it perfectly clear. Sometimes it is not found there. A writer may delay the Step 1 statement, either for suspense or to avoid beginning with an assertion that might make a reader angry. And some writers never have a statement of the Step 1 sentence at all; they prefer to provide clues from connectives (Steps 5 and 6), details (Step 4), and organization (Steps 2 and 3) to let readers figure out the Step 1 for themselves.

The reverse-steps approach works for reading difficult material as well as easy. Not only will it improve your understanding of what you read, it will also improve your writing skill as you notice the techniques professional writers use.

An End and a Beginning

No book can contain all the advice on good writing that good writers and teachers have imparted over the centuries. This book makes no attempt to be so comprehensive. It has focused instead on a few fundamentals that, if applied thoughtfully, make any kind of written communication notably clear and effective.

If there is any final impression this book should leave, it is that effective writing is not a matter of acquiring a mysterious feel for language, nor is it a matter of memorizing a bookful of petty rules. If you happen to have a mysteriously graceful way of using words, so much the better. But what counts most is thinking and common sense.

It boils down to this:

Have something to say. Say it. (Step 1.) Keep to that point. (Steps 2 and 3). Explain it in detail. (Step 4.) Indicate to your reader how your points and details connect. (Steps 5 and 6).

There may be an occasion (perhaps in making a political speech, or getting out of a jam) when you want to write mysteriously, to avoid making a clear point, to hold back from giving an explanation or supporting detail, to omit connections. Then you will know how to do that, too: Write about a topic, not a point; keep any explanation abstract and general. Don't make connections. If your audience wants to ignore reality, that may satisfy them.

But in any case, keep the six steps in mind. Follow them or not, depending on your purposes, but know what you are doing. You have learned not just to write but to make sense.

Exercise

Exercise 10.1. Analyze an article or essay by applying the six steps in reverse as described in this chapter. Circle the connective words (words that connect ideas in Steps 5 and 6). Write *Step 4* in the margin beside each example, anecdote, or detailed statement of fact in a paragraph. Underline three or four subpoints (Step 2). And put a double underline under the main point (Step 1), or if there is no single sentence expressing the main point, write a suitable Step 1 sentence yourself at the top of the first page.

Appendix 1: The Six Steps

STEP 1: Write a sentence stating an opinion that will require further explanation. (Page 16)

STEP 2: Write three or four additional sentences explaining how or why the Step 1 sentence is true or correct. To explain how, give examples, parts of the whole, sequence or chronology; to explain why, give reasons (causes). (Page 24)

STEP 3: Write four or more additional sentences about each of the three or four sentences of Step 2. Conclude the theme with a rounding-off sentence in a separate paragraph. (Page 35)

STEP 4: Go into detail in the four or more sentences of Step 3. Make them as specific as possible. Make them concrete. Use examples and facts. Say a lot about a little, not a little about a lot. (Page 44)

STEP 5: Change the first sentence of each new paragraph, starting with paragraph 2, so that it connects with the paragraph before it. Add key words to connect topics and connective words to connect ideas. (Page 60)

STEP 6: Make sure every sentence is connected to the one before it: by a pronoun, key word or associated word to connect the topic; by a connective word to connect the ideas, or by both. (Page 69)

Appendix 2: Step 2 Examples

The following sentences illustrate the variety of development possible for a single Step 1 thesis: *Chicago is tough.*

Step 2 sentences giving examples:

X Chicago is tough.
1. Chicago people are tough.
2. Chicago traffic is tough.
3. Chicago weather is tough.

X Chicago is tough.
1. The Chicago neighborhood of Englewood is tough.
2. The Chicago neighborhood of Hyde Park is tough.
3. The Chicago neighborhood of Humboldt Park is tough.

X Chicago is tough.
1. Chicago is tough on people who live there.
2. Chicago is tough on people who visit.
3. Chicago is tough on their pets.

Step 2 sentences giving parts of the whole:

X Chicago is tough.
1. The North Side is tough.
2. The West Side is tough.
3. The South Side is tough.
4. Downtown is tough.

Step 2 sentences giving sequence:

X Chicago is tough.
1. Chicago is tough by day.
2. Chicago is tough in the evening.
3. Chicago is tough at night.

Step 2 sentences giving chronology:

X Chicago has always been tough.
1. Chicago was tough in the early 19th century.
2. Chicago was tough in the late 19th century.
3. Chicago was tough in the 20th century.
4. Chicago has been tough so far in the 21st century.

Step 2 sentences giving reasons:

X Chicago is tough.
1. Chicago is tough because my father was shot there.
2. Chicago is tough because my mother had her car stolen there.
3. Chicago is tough because my brother was mugged there.

X Chicago is tough.
1. Chicago is tough because its opportunities have attracted tough people.
2. Chicago is tough because it has been wide open to competition.
3. Chicago is tough because its inhabitants have a romantic belief in the tough poetry of Carl Sandburg and the tough writing of authors like Theodore Dreiser, James T. Farrell, and Nelson Algren.

Appendix 3: Types of Connectives
(See Chapter 6)

Type A: Connecting Topics

1. In the second of any two sentences, use a pronoun or other pro-word to refer to someone or something in the previous sentence. (Page 71.)

2. Repeat a key word or words. (Page 72.)

3. Use a synonym. (Page 72.)

4. Use an antonym. (Page 73.)

5. Use an associated word. (Page 73.)

6. Repeat a sentence structure. (Page 73.)

Type B: Connecting Ideas with Connective Words

1. **Addition**—and, also, too, additionally, in addition, moreover, likewise, similarly, furthermore, as well as, along with, another, again, besides, in the same way; not only . . . but also; next; first, second, third, etc. (Pages 61 and 75.)

2. **Example**—for example, for instance, as an example, as a sample, to illustrate, such as, etc. (Page 75.)

3. **Identity (restatement)**—that is, in other words, to put it another way, to be exact, I mean,, in short, etc. (Page 76.)

4. **Opposite (contrast)**—but, yet, however, nevertheless, nonetheless, notwithstanding, still, though, although, on the contrary, whereas, in contrast, rather, instead, etc. (Page 76; Chapter 8, page 97.)

5. **Cause and effect**—therefore, so, consequently, accordingly, thus, then, as a result, hence, it follows that, because, since, etc. (Page 76.)

6. **Concession (presenting the other side)**—true, granted, admittedly, of course, naturally, unfortunately, some people say (or believe), it could be argued that, it is said, it has been falsely claimed,, we have been told that, etc. (Page 77; Chapter 9, page 102.)

7. **Focusing**—now, indeed, in fact, well, anyhow, etc. (Page 77.)

Appendix 4: Principles of Style
(See Chapter 7)

The way something is written should reflect its meaning: form should follow function. (Page 85)

Do not hesitate to repeat key words. (Page 87)

Keep to the same grammatical subject. (Page 88)

Achieve variety not by changing vocabulary but by making every third sentence or so noticeably longer than the others, and starting every third sentence or so with something other than the grammatical subject. (Page 90)

Appendix 5: Six Rules for Contrast
(See Chapter 8)

In a contrast theme:

1. Make a specific Step 1 statement. Do not just say that two objects or persons are different; say what the basic difference is. (Page 94)

2. Select significant differences, not trivial ones. (Page 95)

3. Include only material that relates to the contrast. (Page 95)

4. If you mention something about one object or person, mention the contrasting thing about the other. (Page 96)

5. Take up things in the order in which you first present them. (Page 96)

6. Indicate contrasts with connective words that signal opposite ideas. (Page 97; see Chapter 6, page 76)

Appendix 6: Rule for Argumentation
(See Chapter 9)

To consider two sides of an issue, conclude your theme with a paragraph that presents the best argument for the other side, followed by a paragraph that replies to that argument.

Finish as usual with a rounding-off sentence that restates your point. (Page 100)

Appendix 7: Reading for the Point
(See Chapter 10, pages 114-115)

1. Look for the connections the author has made (Steps 5 and 6), especially the use of connective words to show the connection of ideas and the author's attitude toward them.

2. Look for the evidence—details, examples, facts—that the author has provided (Steps 3 and 4). What material gets the most attention and detail?

3. Look for the main subpoints (Step 2)—statements that summarize paragraphs, that tell the meaning of different items of evidence.

4. Look for a sentence that summarizes the entire work (Step 1)—that covers all the subpoints and all the evidence. If there is no such sentence in the work, write one yourself.

Index